How Ethical Systems Change: Abortion and Neonatal Care

Sheldon Ekland-Olson and Elyshia Aseltine

Roe v. Wade came like a bolt from the blue, but support had been building for years. For many, the idea that life in the womb was not fully protected under the Constitution was simply not acceptable. Political campaigns were organized and protests launched, including the bombing of clinics and the killing of abortion providers. Questions about the protection and support of life continued after birth. This book is based on a hugely popular undergraduate course taught at The University of Texas, and is ideal for those interested in the social construction of social worth, social problems, and social movements.

Sheldon Ekland-Olson joined The University of Texas at Austin after completing his graduate work at the University of Washington in Seattle and Yale Law School. He is currently the Bernard and Audre Rapoport Centennial Professor of Liberal Arts. He served for five years as Dean of the College of Liberal Arts and then for eight years as Executive Vice President and Provost of the university. He has authored or co-authored several books and numerous articles on criminal justice, prison reform, and capital punishment. Widely recognized for his commitment to teaching undergraduates, he is the recipient of numerous teaching awards. His current interests are reflected in the book *Who Lives, Who Dies, Who Decides?* (Routledge, 2012).

Elyshia Aseltine is an Assistant Professor of Criminal Justice and Criminology at Lycoming College in Williamsport, Pennsylvania. She joined the Lycoming faculty after completing her graduate work in sociology at The University of Texas at Austin. Her research focuses on punishment and inequality in the United States and Africa.

 **University Readers** Reading Materials Evolved.

THE SOCIAL ISSUES COLLECTION™

 **Routledge** Taylor & Francis Group

Framing 21st Century Social Issues

The goal of this new, unique Series is to offer readable, teachable "thinking frames" on today's social problems and social issues by leading scholars. These are available for view on http://routledge.customgateway.com/routledge-social-issues.html.

For instructors teaching a wide range of courses in the social sciences, the Routledge *Social Issues Collection* now offers the best of both worlds: originally written short texts that provide "overviews" to important social issues *as well as* teachable excerpts from larger works previously published by Routledge and other presses.

As an instructor, click to the website to view the library and decide how to build your custom anthology and which thinking frames to assign. Students can choose to receive the assigned materials in print and/or electronic formats at an affordable price.

Available

Body Problems
Running and Living Long in a Fast-Food Society
Ben Agger

Sex, Drugs, and Death
Addressing Youth Problems in American Society
Tammy Anderson

The Stupidity Epidemic
Worrying About Students, Schools, and America's Future
Joel Best

Empire Versus Democracy
The Triumph of Corporate and Military Power
Carl Boggs

Contentious Identities
Ethnic, Religious, and Nationalist Conflicts in Today's World
Daniel Chirot

The Future of Higher Education
Dan Clawson and Max Page

Waste and Consumption
Capitalism, the Environment, and the Life of Things
Simonetta Falasca-Zamponi

Rapid Climate Change
Causes, Consequences, and Solutions
Scott G. McNall

The Problem of Emotions in Societies
Jonathan H. Turner

Outsourcing the Womb
Race, Class, and Gestational Surrogacy in a Global Market
France Winddance Twine

Changing Times for Black Professionals
Adia Harvey Wingfield

How Ethical Systems Change: Abortion and Neonatal Care

Sheldon Ekland-Olson
The University of Texas at Austin

Elyshia Aseltine
Lycoming College

Routledge
Taylor & Francis Group

NEW YORK AND LONDON

First published 2012
by Routledge
711 Third Avenue, New York, NY 10017

Simultaneously published in the UK
by Routledge
2 Park Square, Milton Park, Abingdon, Oxon OX14 4RN

Routledge is an imprint of the Taylor & Francis Group, an informa business

Library of Congress Cataloging in Publication Date
Ekland-Olson, Sheldon, 1944–
How ethical systems change : abortion and neonatal care / Sheldon Ekland-Olson,
Elyshia Aseltine.
p. cm. — (Framing 21st century social issues)
1. Abortion—Moral and ethical aspects—United States. 2. Abortion—Law and
legislation—United States. I. Aseltine, Elyshia. II. Title.
HQ767.15.E35 2011
179.7'6—dc23
2011033466

ISBN13: 978-0-415-50449-2 (pbk)
ISBN13: 978-0-203-12825-1 (ebk)

Typeset in Garamond and Gill Sans
by EvS Communication Networx, Inc.

Printed and bound in the United States of America on acid-free paper.

University Readers (www.universityreaders.com): Since 1992, University
Readers has been a leading custom publishing service, providing reasonably priced,
copyright-cleared, course packs, custom textbooks, and custom publishing services
in print and digital formats to thousands of professors nationwide. The Routledge
Custom Gateway provides easy access to thousands of readings from hundreds of
books and articles via an online library. The partnership of University Readers and
Routledge brings custom publishing expertise and deep academic content together
to help professors create perfect course materials that is affordable for students.

Contents

Series Foreword

The world in the early 21st century is beset with problems—a troubled economy, global warming, oil spills, religious and national conflict, poverty, HIV, health problems associated with sedentary lifestyles. Virtually no nation is exempt, and everyone, even in affluent countries, feels the impact of these global issues.

Since its inception in the 19th century, sociology has been the academic discipline dedicated to analyzing social problems. It is still so today. Sociologists offer not only diagnoses; they glimpse solutions, which they then offer to policy makers and citizens who work for a better world. Sociology played a major role in the civil rights movement during the 1960s in helping us to understand racial inequalities and prejudice, and it can play a major role today as we grapple with old and new issues.

This series builds on the giants of sociology, such as Weber, Durkheim, Marx, Parsons, Mills. It uses their frames, and newer ones, to focus on particular issues of contemporary concern. These books are about the nuts and bolts of social problems, but they are equally about the frames through which we analyze these problems. It is clear by now that there is no single correct way to view the world, but only paradigms, models, which function as lenses through which we peer. For example, in analyzing oil spills and environmental pollution, we can use a frame that views such outcomes as unfortunate results of a reasonable effort to harvest fossil fuels. "Drill, baby, drill" sometimes involves certain costs as pipelines rupture and oil spews forth. Or we could analyze these environmental crises as inevitable outcomes of our effort to dominate nature in the interest of profit. The first frame would solve oil spills with better environmental protection measures and clean-ups, while the second frame would attempt to prevent them altogether, perhaps shifting away from the use of petroleum and natural gas and toward alternative energies that are "green."

These books introduce various frames such as these for viewing social problems. They also highlight debates between social scientists who frame problems differently. The books suggest solutions, both on the macro and micro levels. That is, they suggest what new policies might entail, and they also identify ways in which people, from the ground level, can work toward a better world, changing themselves and their lives and families and providing models of change for others.

Readers do not need an extensive background in academic sociology to benefit from these books. Each book is student-friendly in that we provide glossaries of terms for the uninitiated that are keyed to bolded terms in the text. Each chapter ends with questions for further thought and discussion. The level of each book is accessible to undergraduate students, even as these books offer sophisticated and innovative analyses.

Sheldon Ekland-Olson and his coauthors offer a fascinating four-volume analysis of the evolution of moral, ethical, and legal systems. In each volume, three themes reappear: there are important links between advances in science, technology, and evolving moral, ethical, and legal thinking; crystallizing events clarify issues and motivate reform; and boundaries of social worth are drawn when protecting and supporting life and when resolving dilemmas where the protection of life clashes with the alleviation of suffering.

In this book, Ekland-Olson and Elyshia Aseltine trace how laws preventing the use and distribution of contraception gave rise to a constitutional assertion of individual autonomy and a right to privacy. When coupled with two troubling events involving the potential suffering of the yet-to-be-born, this right formed the foundation for a landmark abortion decision. Implicit in the idea of legal abortion is the assertion that the fetus is not a fully protected person. This assertion was offensive to many and gave rise to a powerful pro-life social movement, elements of which justified the taking of life from abortion providers to protect life of the unborn. As events unfolded the debate continued well into the early months of life. Medical advances facilitated prolonging life of newborns, formerly labeled monstrosities at birth, even in the face of suffering and futility. The quality of these short lives raised the question of whether the quality of life was really worthy of protection and support.

Preface

In the United States no issue more dominated the political landscape in the late 20th century than abortion. The debates were contentious, filled with accusations, and inflamed with violence. They were anchored in a Supreme Court decision, *Roe v. Wade* (1973), For many, *Roe* came like a bolt from the blue. How could justices on the Supreme Court of the United States rule that a fetus was not a fully protected person under the constitution? Such a finding flew in the face of the idea that life is sacred and should be protected.

While its impact was abrupt, the *Roe* decision had been taking shape for many years. Early abortion laws of the 19th century were designed to protect the health of the mother as much as the life of the fetus. Medical practice and available antibiotics had changed this. By mid-20th century, having an abortion, if properly administered, was safer than giving birth after carrying a child to full term. When it came to the risks inherent in having an abortion, it was argued, there was no longer any compelling reason for state intervention.

In addition, following World War II and especially in the decade preceding *Roe*, there were increasing pressures to reaffirm the autonomy of individual choice and to assert the equality of women across the political, social, and legal landscape. The story of a young woman in Arizona, denied an abortion, even though she had taken a drug that all but ensured the recently conceived fetus in her womb would develop serious disabilities and potentially lead a life filled with suffering, drew the nation's attention. At the same time, a rubella pandemic broke out, spreading a disease also associated with serious birth defects. Many wondered, under such circumstances why would we not allow parents to make the heart-wrenching choice to terminate a pregnancy? Was not the alleviation of suffering also a basic human value? Existing laws prohibiting abortion were a travesty.

In this way, values aimed at affirming individual autonomy and the alleviation of suffering came to clash with values asserting the intrinsic value of life. Battle lines were drawn. Politicians took positions, waged campaigns, won and lost elections. Scholars worried over the fine points of philosophical and legal arguments. Activists produced statistics, argued for the rights of the disabled, underscored the importance of privacy and choice, organized right-to-life demonstrations, bombed clinics, and murdered abortion providers. Throughout, an erratic pendulum-like swing of law, policy, and opinion, energized by the tensions of moral dilemmas and the boundaries of protected life was generated.

These debates were not restricted to life in the womb. By mid-20th century, improved medical technologies and procedures had also made it possible to prolong the lives of infants who, only a few short years earlier, had been routinely labeled monstrosities at birth and allowed to die, even hastened along their way. With improved medical capabilities, this changed, as did the surrounding rhetoric. Monstrosities at birth became imperiled infants. Questions were raised about whether parents should be able to refuse available treatments for their recently born child. Turned around, if medical treatments were deemed futile, should doctors be empowered to refuse to treat an infant, even in the face of parental requests to so? Again the debates were heated, heart wrenching, and prolonged.

As this book goes to press, these debates continue. Where should the protective boundaries of life should be placed, what levels of suffering should be tolerated, and who should decide these matters in the early moments and months of life?

1: What Lies Ahead

T his volume is one of four taken from a more detailed treatment in *Who Lives, Who Dies, Who Decides?* (Ekland-Olson 2012). In each of the volumes, the focus is upon two deeply important moral imperatives: Life is sacred and should be protected. Suffering, once detected, should be alleviated. We ask one question: How do we go about justifying the violation of these deeply important, perhaps universal, **moral imperatives**, while holding tightly to their importance?

The short answer is this: With empathy and logic we draw boundaries and resolve dilemmas. From time to time science, technology, and **crystallizing events** disturb, clarify, and inform existing understandings, calling for new resolutions of dilemmas and definitions of life's protective boundaries. In this manner moral systems evolve. They do so along a jagged and often contentious path.

In this volume we wind our way through the debates infusing the boundaries and dilemmas of the early moments and months of life. Where are the boundaries of protected life to be drawn—prior to conception, at conception, at viability, inches from life? In the early months following birth, the protection of life and the alleviation of suffering sometimes conflict. Some infant lives, some moments early in life are deemed more worthy of protection and support than others. Deep disagreements are found. Who should decide?

Widely divergent answers have been proposed. These answers have been shaped by religious and political beliefs as well as practices among physicians, sometimes hidden from public view. Political campaigns and social movements have been launched, up to and including the bombing of abortion clinics and the killing of abortion providers. These lethal actions have paradoxically been justified by a commitment to protect and support life. The cycle is completed when those killing abortion providers are themselves executed, again justified through a commitment to protect and support life.

From time to time high-profile events have drawn attention, crystallized thought, and galvanized action. In the early 1960s an Arizona law prevented a young mother with four children from obtaining an abortion, even though she had taken a drug associated with severe life-limiting, resource-draining birth defects. Almost simultaneously, a rubella pandemic raised similar issues among a much large number of expectant mothers. For many, then existing laws prohibiting abortion were a tragic injustice. They increased the chances of defective births as well as the deaths of mothers seeking illegal abortions in unsanitary conditions.

A decade later, a Supreme Court decision came like a "bolt from the blue." It declared that a fetus was not a fully protected person under the Constitution and that there were important rights to privacy protecting the mother's choice to have an abortion. For many, this was unconscionable. Shortly thereafter a pro-life movement expanded, a former abortion provider, using newly available ultrasound images to show what was said to be the "silent scream" of a fetus being aborted, produced a film. President Reagan distributed the film to Congress. It was shown in churches and discussed in the media. Other even more jarring images were produced that galvanized action, sometimes lethal.

In 1991, what came to be known as the Summer of Mercy called attention to second- and third-term abortions. Emotional political campaigns continued, clinics were bombed, and abortion providers killed. A little over a decade later, federal legislation outlawed "partial birth abortions," similar to those that so concerned the Summer of Mercy protesters. This law was a strange and strained piece of legislation. It limited the taking of life in late term pregnancy, not in principle but by the vaginal location of the fetus. Procedures adapted to meet the anatomical requirements of the new law. Late-term abortions continued. More recent attempts have been made to limit late term abortions based on the argument that the fetus can experience pain. The physician targeted by Summer of Mercy protesters, also known as "Tiller the Baby Killer," was shot to death while worshipping at his church on Sunday May 31, 2009. Dr. Tiller's murder was justified by the assailant's supporters through reference to biblical scripture calling for the protection of life.

The debates over life and death decisions in the early moments and months of life have not been limited to life in the womb. For many years, there was no known way to prolong the lives of infants labeled "monstrosities at birth." With advances in medical technology, this changed. New decisions arose, rhetoric changed and monstrosities at birth became imperiled infants. Issues coalesced when a young infant, diagnosed with Down Syndrome, was allowed to die when his parents refused permission to perform a relatively simple operation. Many were appalled. Such infants, it was argued, deserved protection. New regulations were put in place. These hastily crafted policies failed to account for many more difficult circumstances when the infant's life was infused with far greater suffering and when medical treatment seemed futile. Additional tragic stories came to light. Further clarification ensued.

Even with this clarification, however, uncertainty remained. Where are the protective boundaries of meaningful life to be drawn? What are the boundaries of tolerable suffering? What should be done when the protection of life and the alleviation of suffering compete? Who should decide? The power of unavoidable moral dilemmas to infuse the uncertainties of life with tension is nowhere more evident than in the early moments and months of life.

II: A Bolt from the Blue

Abortion Is Legalized

W hen does abortion become infanticide? Drawn less starkly, when does life possess properties that bring it under the "life is sacred and should be protected" umbrella? Given the high probability of disagreement, who should decide?

Many answers have been given to these now familiar questions. Religions have evolved beliefs, legislatures have passed laws, courts have articulated findings, and individuals have made choices. Politicians have taken positions, waged campaigns, won and lost elections. Scholars have worried over the fine points of philosophical and legal arguments. Activists have produced statistics, argued for the rights of the disabled, underscored the importance of privacy and choice, organized right-to-life demonstrations, bombed clinics, and murdered abortion providers. Throughout, an erratic pendulum-like swing of law, policy, and opinion, energized by the tensions of moral dilemmas and disagreements over whether all stages of human life are equally worthy of protection and support has been generated.

The most encompassing of all boundaries are those flowing from the idea that all life, at least all human life, is intrinsically, equally, and deeply important. There are no lives, no moments of life more worthy of protection than others. The boundaries of protected life do not even necessarily attach to individual human beings. Instead, they define protections of *LIFE* writ large. "Something is intrinsically valuable…if its value is *independent* of what people happen to enjoy or want or need or what is good for them…. Something is sacred or inviolable when its deliberate destruction would dishonor what ought to be honored" (Dworkin 1993: 71). Such a view produces a very broad umbrella of protection. It anchors the Catholic Church's rationale for the regulation of contraception.

> (E)ach and every marital act must of necessity retain its intrinsic relationship to the procreation of human life … We are obliged once more to declare that the direct interruption of the generative process already begun … (is) to be absolutely excluded as lawful means of regulating the number of children. Equally to be condemned, as the magisterium of the Church has affirmed on many occasions, is direct sterilization, whether of the man or of the woman, whether permanent or

temporary.... Similarly excluded is any action which either before, at the moment of, or after sexual intercourse, is specifically intended to prevent procreation—whether as an end or as a means.

(Pope Paul VI 1968)

If laws were grounded in this theocratic proscription, there could be little doubt. *LIFE*, even *before* conception, would be protected. Even voluntary contraceptive measures of all kinds would be illegal. Not so long ago, throughout much of the United States, they were.

From Comstockery to the Right to Privacy

In the early 1870s Anthony Comstock, began a crusade. He became a quintessential moral entrepreneur (Becker 1963). Comstock was offended by readily available material he considered obscene, material which included explicit advertisements for various birth control measures. These threatened the public good. A law was needed. In 1872 Comstock completed his model legislation and traveled to Washington D.C. By March of 1873, using Comstock's template, Congress passed a federal law, an Act for the Suppression of Trade in, and Circulation of, Obscene Literature and Articles for Immoral Use. It would eventually become known simply as the Comstock Law.

Within a few years, a majority of states had passed similar laws. One of the stricter versions came in 1879 in Connecticut, Comstock's home state. Here, even married couples were vulnerable to a jail term for the use of birth control. While difficult to enforce, especially when it came to the use of birth control methods, these efforts almost immediately gave rise to counter crusades and crusaders, such as the birth control movement and another moral entrepreneur, the enigmatic Margaret Sanger (Katz, Hajo, and Engelman 2003). Sanger, is credited with founding the American Birth Control Movement, which eventually evolved into the Planned Parenthood Federation of America. Driven by a sense of injustice and the repression of women, Sanger and those committed to the increased availability of birth control methods challenged, even to the point of going to jail, the legitimacy of the Comstock laws.

For Sanger and her colleagues, these statutes allowed inappropriate governmental intrusion into the private lives of citizens. They manifested long-standing inequality for women and the repression of their ability to control their bodies and enjoy their lives. For Sanger and those who agreed, the case was clear. Persons should be able to plan their families effectively. In the 1930s, when the severe economic consequences of the Great Depression were felt, these arguments became ever more persuasive. Controlling the number of children became increasingly important and the pressure challenging the legitimacy of the Comstock Laws increased.

As demand for contraception grew, the market responded. Research and development operations of pharmaceutical companies expanded. Eventually, what came to be known simply as The Pill was developed. An early version, Enovid, was approved for the U.S. market for the regulation of menses in the late 1950s. In 1960 it was submitted to the Food and Drug Administration and approved as a birth control pill. The approval of Enovid, along with numerous other birth control drugs that followed, marked a dramatic improvement in both effectiveness and convenience of birth control options. Given this increased effectiveness and convenience, as well as the profits that could be made, challenges to State intervention began in earnest.

For a few years the legal structure continued to lag behind these innovations, but not for long. A version of the 1879 Connecticut Comstock statute remained on the books. Executive Director of the Planned Parenthood League of Connecticut, Estelle Griswold, along with her medical director, Lee Buxton, a member of the Department of Obstetrics and Gynecology at Yale Medical School, gave a married couple information and medical advice on how to prevent conception. It was against the law. They were convicted. They appealed their conviction, and eventually their case was argued before the Supreme Court in March of 1965 in *Griswold v. Connecticut* (1965). A little over two months later the birth control prohibitions of a Connecticut statute, grounded in almost century-old legislation, were declared unconstitutional.

For most this was an easy case. All nine of the Supreme Court justices, even those dissenting with the decision, saw the cultural lag in existing laws and agreed this anti-contraception statute was not wise, and, in the words of Justice Stewart, writing in dissent, even "silly" and "asinine." Nowhere in the Constitution, however, is birth control mentioned. Nowhere in the Bill of Rights are there references to family planning. Assuming that any decision by the Supreme Court would need to be anchored in the Constitution, not personal beliefs, where should the justices look? Penumbras, or shadowed implications of general principles, were the answer. "(T)he Bill of Rights" Justice Douglas argued for the majority in *Griswold*, "have penumbras, formed by emanations from those guarantees that help give them life and substance." In particular, the Court had found protections of individual autonomy embedded in the not precisely articulated implications the First, Fourth, Fifth, Ninth, and Fourteenth Amendments. The common penumbral collection point, Justice Douglas argued, was the right to privacy. Whatever the roots of his reasoning, the majority of the Court found the sweep of the Connecticut statute unnecessarily broad. Married couples should have the right to choose to use contraceptive measures. Laws prohibiting such practices were unconstitutional.

In a case decided some seven years later in Massachusetts (*Eisenstadt v. Baird* 1972), this right was extended, for reasons of equity, to unmarried persons as well. In this case William Baird had been convicted of two offenses committed while lecturing on contraception to an audience at Boston University. He had exhibited contraceptive articles and at the end of the lecture had given a package of Emko vaginal foam to a young woman in the audience. By so doing, he was in violation of Massachusetts' law.

Baird's convictions were appealed. The Supreme Court's rationale for overturning the conviction was straightforward.

> If under *Griswold* the distribution of contraceptives to married persons cannot be prohibited, a ban on distribution to unmarried persons would be equally impermissible. It is true that in *Griswold* the right of privacy in question inhered in the marital relationship. Yet the marital couple is not an independent entity with a mind and heart of its own, but an association of two individuals each with a separate intellectual and emotional makeup. If the right of privacy means anything, it is the right of the individual, married or single, to be *free from unwarranted governmental intrusion into matters so fundamentally affecting a person as the decision whether to bear or beget a child.*
>
> (*Eisenstadt v. Baird* 1972; emphasis added)

With these two Supreme Court decisions victory could be declared. New England had been the region of the country with the most stringent Comstock laws. These laws were now dead. The boundaries of *LIFE* protected by the community's legal system did not extend prior to conception to choices regarding contraception. In addition, and importantly, to those paying attention, the last sentence in the above excerpt was important. The stage was set to restrict governmental intrusion even further. Privacy was now said to extend to the decision to "bear or beget a child."

Legal scholars would continue to argue over whether privacy could be found in the penumbras of constitutional language, but for most citizens the articulated restrictions on governmental intrusion when it came to contraception seemed quite reasonable. There were realms of individual autonomy and dignity into which the government should not intrude. Now the question became, was the decision to terminate pregnancy in the same category? Here, there was far less consensus.

While privacy and the right to choose are important, very few argue they are absolute. How far does the right to privacy extend and where does the autonomy and sanctity of the newly forming life with associated protections begin? At what point does state intrusion become compelling? Knowing that many fertilized embryos will be destroyed, should *in vitro* fertilization be prohibited? Knowing also that research on stem cells may lead to a cure for debilitating diseases, can parents decide to donate their sperm and ova to produce very early stage **blastocysts** for this purpose? Given improved abilities to genetically detect diseases or disabilities, do parents have the right to terminate pregnancy for quality of life reasons, even in the middle and late stages of gestation? Since parents have the legal responsibility to feed, nurture, and protect their children, should the State step in if a mother drinks excessively or takes drugs knowing in all likelihood her behavior will damage the mental and physical well being of her not-yet-born child? Can parents of a newborn with a life threatening illness simply decide to withhold treatment and let the child starve to death? These and other questions would dominate political debates in the years just ahead.

Potential for Life, Potential for Suffering

The Court's conclusions regarding privacy, anchored in penumbras of constitutional language or not, were not reached in a vacuum. Importantly, a broad-based civil rights movement designed to establish a more equitable standing for women was gaining momentum. In addition, stunning advances in understanding the process of reproduction and mapping the structure of genetic material were being secured. Techniques to observe and understand intrauterine developments were being improved. Justices on the Supreme Court were clearly aware of these events. They were also aware of heightened concerns about the potential quality of life for the yet-to-be-born. These concerns were intensified first by the side effects of the drug Thalidomide and then by a pandemic of "German Measles" associated with what came to be known as Congenital Rubella Syndrome. Alleviation of the potential suffering of the yet-to-be-born would collide with the imperative to protect potential life. People chose sides, advocates were advancing their cause.

Stories of these events have been often told. They shaped public opinion. Given their significance, they are worth repeating. In 1962 Sherri Finkbine was the host of a Phoenix-based edition of the popular children's show, *Romper Room*. She was also the mother of four children under the age of seven and pregnant with what would be her fifth child. Early in her pregnancy, she had been taking a drug her husband, a local high-school teacher, had purchased on a trip to London to help her sleep and deal with morning sickness. This drug turned out to be the strongest possible dosage of Thalidomide. When she became aware that Thalidomide might be associated with very serious crippling birth defects, she went to her doctor for advice. He "firmly" suggested that she have a therapeutic abortion. As she later recalled, "In talking it over with my [obstetrician], he said, 'Sherri, if you were my own wife and we two had four small children, and you really wanted a fifth child, I'd say start again next month under better odds'" (Luker 1984: 62–65).

At that time in Arizona, early-term abortions were available through a walking-on-the-edge-of-the-law interpretation of the Arizona statute wherein the woman's physician agreed that abortion was appropriate and a three-member therapeutic abortion board at the hospital concurred. While her doctor recommended against going to a local Catholic hospital where her last baby had been born, he was confident that approval would be a mere formality at a local public hospital. It was. The procedure was scheduled for the next Monday morning.

Fearing that other families might also purchase the drug as her husband had done, Finkbine decided to call a friend who worked for the local newspaper to relate her story and alert others. Monday morning the bold headline read, "Baby-Deforming Drug May Cost Woman Her Child Here." Reading the headline and recognizing that their approval of this as well as many other therapeutic abortions might violate any strict reading of the Arizona statute, hospital doctors and administrators immediately cancelled the scheduled procedure.

What initially promised to be an almost automatic approval soon became something quite different. The national wire services picked up the story. Prominent papers across the country as well as the international press ran features. Sherri and her husband received thousands of letters. Death threats were made and FBI protection for the Finkbines was secured. Eventually, Sherri Finkbine was granted permission to go to Sweden where she had an abortion in the fourth month of her pregnancy. There the doctor reported the fetus was so seriously deformed it would not have survived. In the aftermath, both Sherri and her husband lost their jobs, Sherri being told by the vice president of the NBC affiliate that she was no longer fit to handle children (Risen and Thomas 1998).

By all accounts, this heart-wrenching, widely publicized case marked an important turning point. As one author, echoed by many others, put it, the refusal to grant a legal abortion in these dramatic conditions, marked a point "when a diffuse dissatisfaction with the law began to crystallize into an organized movement to change the law" (Sauer 1974: 55).

Further impetus for change came from another unexpected source. Rubella or "German Measles" had been recognized for more than 200 years (Nicholas 2000). In the early 1940s, it had been linked to a wide range of abnormalities including congenital heart defects, deafness, cataracts and glaucoma, and severe to moderate psychomotor retardation, along with a mortality rate approaching 10 percent to 15 percent. Epidemics of rubella seemed to occur on an irregular cycle of six to nine years. A large-scale pandemic swept across Europe and the United States between 1964 and 1966. Estimates of the impact found their way to 1969 Senate hearings (Apgar 1969) and indicated that in the United States there had been some 50,000 abnormal pregnancies, including 20,000 newborns with birth defects and something on the order of 30,000 fetal deaths.

The issue came to a head in 1966 when a member of the California Board of Medical Examiners, who had taken a strong stance against abortion, initiated proceedings to revoke the licenses of nine prominent, well-respected San Francisco physicians who had been performing abortions for mothers exposed to rubella. Their actions were contrary to an almost century-old California statute rooted in Comstock-era legislation (Joffe, Weitz, and Stacey 2004). Faced with the loss of their licenses, a spokesman for the physicians, who came to be known as the "San Francisco Nine," questioned the law's legitimacy based on their professional responsibilities. "We do not believe that violation of an archaic statue is unprofessional conduct" (Dynek 1963). The issue had been building for some time.

A Social Movement Splinters

In the 1950s, concerned physicians and Planned Parenthood joined hands with a group of legal scholars to draft a model abortion statute as part of the American Law Institute's Model Penal Code (MPC) initiative (Halfmann 2003; Kadish 1999). The Comstock Laws were only one example of penal codes throughout the country in need of reform. The section of the MPC dealing with abortion was completed in 1959. It provided for abortions when there was substantial risk to the physical or mental health of the pregnant woman, when **congenital defects** were indicated, and when the pregnancy was the result of rape, incest, or "felonious intercourse."

With this model statute in hand, a few states passed new legislation in the early to mid 1960s to allow abortions in the case of rape and when the woman's physical or mental health was at stake. It was, however, the widespread publicity of Sherri Finkbine's experience with Thalidomide along with the threat of birth defects resulting from the rubella outbreak and the resulting move to prosecute nine highly respected physicians that galvanized reform efforts.

Efforts to reform California's Comstock-era abortion statute were initiated in 1961, a year before Sherri Finkbine's struggle with the effects of Thalidomide. A bill was filed, based on the American Law Institute's (ALI) proposal. Hearings were held, but the bill died in committee. Two years later, in the aftermath of the now widespread concern with Thalidomide, the Society for Humane Abortion (SHA) was founded in San Francisco. SHA soon became a well-organized effort to collectively argue for a woman's unbridled right to choose. Leaving the final decision in the hands of individual physicians and hospital therapeutic abortion committees, such as had been done in Arizona, was a mistake. Instead, the SHA argued, "The termination of pregnancy is a decision which the person or family involved should be free to make as their own religious beliefs, values, emotions, and circumstances may dictate" (Reagan 1997: 223–24).

In this manner competing interests among advocates for reform of the abortion laws began to emerge. Women's rights advocates bumped against physicians and others who would leave the decision in the hands of the doctors and therapeutic committees. Members of the SHA were unequivocal in arguing for the primacy of a woman's right to choose. With these competing versions of reform framed, a second round of hearings was held in the California legislature in 1964.

By then the rubella pandemic was at full force. The heart wrenching impact of the Thalidomide tragedies was evident. In counterbalance, the Catholic Church's leadership continued a strong lobbying effort in opposition to abortion in any form. Ironically, they also found strength in the Thalidomide and rubella events. Aren't the lives of all the yet-to-be-born children worthy of protection? Why would the potential for birth defects make a life less valuable? How can one predict how severe a potential birth defect might be? How much would the quality of life the yet-to-be-born suffer?

These are not easy questions. No easy answers were forthcoming. Given competing interest groups—professional, personal, and religious—the 1964 hearings in the California legislature again ended in no formal action, this time following a much more contentious debate. The now heated and divisive political climate surrounding abortion reform in California was mirrored in New York, Colorado, Illinois, and other states.

Previously, physicians had surmised that easing the restrictive physician discretion laws would be relatively straightforward since it would simply formalize existing practices into law. Following the 1964 hearings, however, it was clear that those calling for demand (i.e., abortion for any reason) as well as those adamantly opposed to abortion under any circumstances were generating strong, effective opposition to leaving the decision in the hands of doctors and hospital committees. Organized efforts to advance the interests of physicians and therapeutic abortion committees began to take shape.

Like-minded colleagues supporting a bill patterned after the ALI's physician discretion recommendations decided to convene a meeting. This gathering included professors, lawyers, social workers and public health professionals. Out of these meetings and discussions, the California Committee on Therapeutic Abortions (CCTA) was formed. With carefully crafted statements in hand and a plan of action developed, CCTA launched an initiative to educate the public and solicit support for the Beilenson Bill, named after the sponsoring Beverly Hills state senator, Anthony Beilenson.

This time they were successful. In 1967 the Beilenson Bill passed. It included provisions for physician discretion and the establishment of therapeutic abortion boards. These individuals and boards could consider both the physical and mental health of the woman, and circumstances when the pregnancy was the result of rape or incest, including cases of statutory rape when the woman was below the age of fifteen. Addressing the issue of potential birth defects, all initial versions of the bill also included provisions for the consideration of "fetal indications."

Given that much of the impetus for reform had emerged from the rubella outbreak and the Thalidomide scare, these latter provisions were to be expected. Last-minute negotiations with the governor and his advisers, however, led to the deletion of this portion of the bill. In the end, Governor Ronald Reagan, later known for his adamant anti-abortion stance (Reagan 1983), signed the Beilenson Bill, without the provisions for "fetal indications." With the governor's signature, this bill became one of the most important pieces of abortion legislation to date. As important as this legislation was, counter pressures inherent in the deeply embedded moral dilemmas would not go away. These opposing pressures would be highlighted with the conviction of a doctor who was an active member of CCTA.

A Bolt from the Blue

Even as the Beilenson Bill was being crafted, debated, and passed, an abortion case was winding its way to the California Supreme Court. A young, then unmarried, woman had become pregnant. She and the father had seen Dr. Leon Belous on television advocating for change in California abortion laws. Dr. Belous was a long-practicing physician specializing in obstetrics and gynecology. He was also a member of the Board of Directors of the California Committee on Therapeutic Abortion. The couple had written down his telephone number from the television show and later called him, asking for assistance in securing an abortion.

After an examination confirmed her pregnancy, the woman and the father of the child pleaded in an emotional office visit with Dr. Belous for assistance. There was no immediate threat to the woman's health. There were no indications of fetal defects. Nevertheless, the couple told the doctor they would secure an abortion, one way or another, even if they had to go to Tijuana, Mexico. Dr. Belous insisted he did not perform abortions, but in response to their continued pleadings and his concern for the mother's health and safety if she went to Tijuana for an abortion, he gave them a telephone number of an acquaintance who performed abortions in a neighboring city. He also gave the woman a prescription for antibiotics and instructed her to return for an examination if she decided to go through with the abortion.

The abortion was performed. As the mother was resting, the police, having been informed that an unlicensed doctor from Mexico was performing abortions, came into the office-apartment to arrest him. In the process, they discovered notebooks containing the names of other patients and numerous physicians, including Dr. Belous. On the basis of this information, they arrested Dr. Belous.

Dr. Belous was convicted after a jury trial in 1967, the same year the Beilenson Bill was passed. He received a $5,000 fine and two years probation. He appealed this decision to the Supreme Court of California. In many ways foreshadowing the U.S. Supreme Court decisions just around the corner, the California court overturned Dr. Belous's conviction, finding the wording of the law "necessary to preserve her life" too vague and uncertain to pass California constitutional muster. They also noted the recent finding in *Griswold* as well as several of their own decisions that protected "right of privacy" or "liberty" in matters related to marriage, family, and sex.

As a final consideration of the state's duty to balance protections of the mother with those of the unborn, the court held "there are major and decisive areas where the embryo and fetus are not treated as equivalent to the born child" and that "the law has always recognized that the pregnant woman's right to life takes precedence over any interest the State may have in the unborn." With these conclusions, the Supreme Court of California became the first in the nation to strike down an abortion statute (*People v. Belous* 1969). It did so in a classic case of **abortion on demand**.

Throughout the 1960s, the collective climate of perceived injustice and the illegitimacy of intrusive state action was strong. It was in this climate, when every public opinion poll indicated a substantial decline in the trust, respect, and perceived legitimacy of governmental actions and policies, that the National Organization for Women (NOW) was launched. NOW, eventually claiming half-a-million members, soon became a rallying point for the women's movement. While the right of a woman to choose to terminate her pregnancy was originally not a central concern NOW addressed, for many it was a cornerstone. As one activist associated with the Society for Humane Abortion reported in a subsequent interview:

> [W]ithout that right, we'd have about as many rights as the cow in the pasture that's taken to the bull once a year. You could give her all those rights, too, but they wouldn't mean anything; if you can't control your own body you can't control your future ...
>
> (Luker 1984: 97)

One of NOW's founders, Betty Friedan, soon became convinced and joined forces with author Lawrence Lader and prominent New York physician Dr. Benard Nathanson. These three high profile advocates for abortion rights helped convene a group of like-minded colleagues, and in 1969 the National Association for the Repeal of Abortion Laws (NARAL), eventually known as NARAL Pro-Choice America, was founded.

Before the founding of NARAL, Lader had published an influential book titled simply, *Abortion*, as well as an earlier well-received biography of Margaret Sanger. Using Sanger as a model, Lader had been one of the architects of the abortion movement's "confrontation politics." This strategy had resulted in a number of arrests including the 1968 arrest of Washington D.C. abortion provider, Dr. Milan Vuitch, whose case eventually came to the Supreme Court. In 1971, one day before the justices agreed to hear *Roe v. Wade* and *Doe v. Bolton*, the Court issued an intentionally crafted compromise in the Vuitch case (Greenhouse 2005: 76–78), finding that the concept of the woman's health included psychological as well as physical well-being and establishing the importance of a physician's professional judgment and discretion in abortion decisions. *United States v. Vuitch,* along with Lader's book, *Abortion,* would be repeatedly cited in the *Roe* and *Doe* decisions.

The third co-founder of NARAL, Bernard Nathanson, was at one time director of the largest abortion clinic in New York City. Perhaps reflecting at a personal level the moral dilemma playing out on the public stage, he became alienated from the practice of abortion and after the *Roe* and *Doe* decisions joined forces with the Right-to-Life movement. He would go on to produce and narrate the widely circulated, and some would claim incendiary, film, *The Silent Scream.*

These personal, professional, and association networks embedded in and bridging across such organizations as ALI, SHA, CCTA, NOW, and NARAL mobilized resources in a nationwide social movement to secure more liberalized abortion laws. By 1972, some 16 states had enacted liberalized abortion statutes based largely on the Model Penal Code of the American Law Institute (Duffy 1971). Four states, including California after the *Belous* case and a subsequent decision in 1972 declaring portions of the 1967 abortion legislation unconstitutional, had statutes allowing for abortion on demand, as long as it was performed by a licensed physician. Many abortion activists were ready to declare, "Mission Accomplished." Except for the political clout of the Catholic Church, the right-to-life advocates had yet to gather counter-balancing effectiveness.

This would change with the Supreme Court's action in *Roe* and *Doe*. What advocates for freedom-of-choice and physician's discretion hailed as a victory had an opposite and galvanizing effect on those who opposed abortion. *Roe* and *Doe* went against everything they believed in. How could the Supreme Court say the Constitution of the United States—THE CONSTITUTION OF THE UNITED STATES!—excluded the unborn child from fully protected persons?

As Kristin Luker notes from her interviews with activists, the mobilizing impact of *Roe* came like a bolt from the blue. More people joined the pro-life movement in 1973 than in any other year, reporting they were moved to do so the very day the decision was handed down (Luker 1984: 137).

These now awakened activists would soon become a force to be reckoned with. They would advance a very different conception of the protected boundaries of life than the Supreme Court had outlined and would draw upon personal and faith-based networks to mobilize resources and build an empathetic identification with the unborn child from the moment of conception. If the law of the land did not protect life, the law of the land was unjust and illegitimate. It needed to be changed, ignored, or intentionally disobeyed. Some went even further, advocating violent action—up to and including the taking of life to protect life. The vehemence of the reaction was unanticipated by the Supreme Court Justices, crafting an opinion to more clearly draw the boundaries around protected life.

DISCUSSION QUESTIONS

1. Describe Comstock Laws and how they regulated contraception use in the United States.
2. Loretta Lynn released a controversial song called "The Pill" in the 1970s. Conduct an Internet search to find the lyrics of the song. What issues does Lynn's song raise about women's reproductive rights?
3. The U.S. Supreme Court argued that the right to privacy can be gleaned from the penumbras of the U.S. Constitution. Describe this right and how it applies to the use of contraception.

4. What is your position on the Sherry Finkbine case? Should the Finkbines have been free to choose to terminate the pregnancy of their Thalidomide-exposed fetus? Why or why not?

5. Assume that abortion is legal and that you are an administrator attempting to draft abortion policies for the hospital. What policies would you propose for your hospital to follow? Consider questions such as: Who is able to make the final choice to terminate a pregnancy? Should the decision reside with the mother? The parents? A physician's committee? What time limits, if any, will your hospital implement on the ability to terminate a pregnancy? What exceptions, if any, will your hospital implement for special circumstances, e.g., pregnancies that are the result of incest or rape, potential birth defects of, health risks to mother, etc.

6. One argument for keeping abortion legal is that women intent on terminating their pregnancies will seek illegal and potentially risky abortions. Do you find this argument compelling? Why or why not?

III: Man's Law or God's Will

W hen *Roe v. Wade*, from Texas, and *Doe v. Bolton*, from Georgia, were originally scheduled for argument before the Supreme Court in 1971 there were only seven sitting justices. For reasons of failing health, two justices had retired in September of that year. As a result, Chief Justice Burger set up a committee to screen cases and recommend which were controversial enough to be postponed until a full nine-member court could be convened, and which could move forward easily with only seven justices participating. Having heard mainly from broad-based, well-organized constituencies favoring liberalized abortion laws, and having been influenced by the searing impact of the Thalidomide tragedies and widespread birth defects resulting from the rubella pandemic, the initial thinking was that the abortion cases before them could be quietly decided on narrow grounds.

In a note written several years later to then Chief Justice Rehnquist, Justice Blackmun recalled his participation on this committee. "I remember that the Old Chief appointed a screening committee, chaired by Potter, to select cases that could (it was assumed) be adequately heard by a Court of seven. I was on that little committee. We did not do a good job. Potter pressed for *Roe v. Wade* and *Doe v. Bolton* to be heard and did so in the misapprehension that they involved nothing more than an application of *Younger v. Harris*. How wrong we were" (Greenhouse 2005: 80).

Landmark Cases Take Shape

Blackmun's original draft of a possible decision in the *Roe* case, written in 1971, ran some 17 pages and concentrated on the relatively narrow question of whether the wording of the Texas statute was too vague. There was no need, Blackmun felt, to consider privacy and the rights of the fetus. This narrowly drawn approach, however, met with opposition from other members of the still seven-justice Court.

A related case from Georgia, *Doe v. Bolton,* was heard at the same time. Whereas the *Roe* case from Texas reflected a law firmly rooted in late 19-century legislation, the case from Georgia was of more recent vintage. It directly reflected recommendations made in 1959 by the American Law Institute. Both cases raised issues of privacy, which had been addressed in several recent Court cases. *Eisenstadt*, in particular and perhaps purposefully, had incorporated wording, "If the right to privacy means anything, it is the right ... to bear or beget a child" (*Griswold v. Connecticut* 1965).

Clearly, this wording had implications for abortion cases such as *Roe* and *Doe*. Given the ensuing discussion among the justices that followed Blackmun's narrowly drawn initial draft, the Court decided to reargue both cases when the Court was at full strength. Eventually, the *Roe* decision, now three times as long as Blackmun's original draft, would be the lead case. It addressed privacy as applied to a woman's right to decide to terminate her pregnancy, the state's dual interest in protecting the life and health of the mother, and the boundaries of protected life for the fetus.

The Court released its *Roe* and *Doe* decisions on January 22, 1973. This date was not accidental. Chief Justice Burger, President Nixon's first appointment to the Court, feared the decision might be a politically embarrassing to the president. He delayed submitting his short concurring opinion until two days before President Nixon was sworn into office for his second term. This delayed the release of the *Roe* and *Doe* decisions until after Inauguration Day (Geeenhouse 2005: 100).

The decisions might have been released, but the controversy remained very much alive. If anything, the *Roe* and *Doe* decisions intensified the debate, set the stage for questioning legitimacy of the law and thereby lit the fuse for violence.

Legitimacy Questioned

A few months after the *Roe* decision, a well-respected Yale law professor, John Hart Ely, sowed the early seeds of questioned legitimacy in an article that became one of the most widely cited pieces in the history of the *Yale Law Journal* (Ely 1973). For Ely, it was not so much what was decided, but who made the decision. The influence of Ely's piece stemmed in part from his thoughtful articulation of his argument. It was further strengthened because he was himself a supporter of abortion rights. "Were I a legislator," Ely wrote, "I would vote for a statute very much like the one the Court ends up drafting" (1973: 926).

The Supreme Court, however, should not be in the business of drafting legislation. To secure legitimacy for their decisions, the Court needed to make a connection with constitutional issues and not ground their findings in personal values or policy preferences. This, Ely argued, had not been done. *Roe* was a bad decision because it was an intrusion by by the Supreme Court into matters best left to the state legislatures.

The majority of justices on the Court, of course, disagreed. Indeed, the Court had anticipated much of Ely's argument in *Roe*:

> We forthwith acknowledge our awareness of the sensitive and emotional nature of the abortion controversy, of the vigorous opposing views, even among physicians, and of the deep and seemingly absolute convictions that the subject inspires. One's philosophy, one's experiences, one's exposure to the raw edges of human existence,

one's religious training, one's attitudes toward life and family and their values, and the moral standards one establishes and seeks to observe, are all likely to influence and to color one's thinking and conclusions about abortion … Our task, of course, is to resolve the issue by constitutional measurement, free of emotion and of predilection. We seek earnestly to do this.

In the years following, there were others, who assessed the decision in much the same way Ely had done. A little over two decades later, the abortion debate had gained intensity. It infused political campaigns. Additional Court decisions had been released. Disagreements over abortion had become part of what some saw as a cultural war (Hunter 1991; see also Fiorina, Abrams, and Pope 2006). A symposium on the topic was published in 1996, by a group of influential scholars in *First Things* (Arkes et al. 1996). Editors of *First Things*, commenting on what they saw as the Supreme Court's abuse of power, were worried.

They wondered whether, "we are witnessing the end of democracy." In even more dramatic terms they continued, "Law, as it is presently made by the judiciary, has declared its independence from morality. Among the most elementary principles of Western Civilization is the truth that laws which violate the moral law are null and void and must in conscience be disobeyed." "What is happening now," the editors continued, "is the displacement of a constitutional order by a regime that does not have, will not obtain, and cannot command the consent of the people." This left the editors wondering "whether we have reached or are reaching the point where conscientious citizens can no longer give moral assent to the existing regime" (Arkes et al. 1996).

These are very serious assertions. For contributors to the symposium, the questioned legitimacy of judicial usurpation of legislative decisions went beyond considerations of abortion, but abortion was the linchpin. As might be expected, such claims generated a good deal of controversy, even among contributors to the symposium and those serving on the editorial advisory board.[1] For some citizens, more removed from the academic fine points being drawn, the case was clear. Driven by an allegiance to a higher law they found in biblical scripture, withdrawal of legitimacy was complete. An unjust law was no law at all. Violence followed.

---

1   One prominent contributor, Robert H. Bork, while standing by his critical analysis, wished the editors had not made their suggestions and noted in a follow-on letter to the editors, "The necessity for reform, even drastic reform, does not call the legitimacy of the entire American 'regime' into question." In another letter to the editors, a member of the *First Things* Editorial Board resigned, suggesting that the editors had "…raised so grave and, in my opinion, irresponsible an issue, and given it such prominence, that I cannot, in good conscience, continue to serve…"

A Clash of Absolutes?

As the battleground of *Roe* and *Doe* took shape, abortion laws then in effect dated mainly from the latter half of the 19th century, with some of more recent origin reflecting the template provided by the Model Penal Code. Over these years, medical advances had been made. Law lagged behind.

When the earlier laws criminalizing abortion were enacted, antiseptic techniques and antibiotics were not widely used or available. It could be argued, indeed it was argued, that the real focus of these early criminal abortion laws was not to protect the unborn. Rather they were designed to protect the life of the pregnant woman.

As the *Roe* Court put it:

> The State has a legitimate interest in seeing to it that abortion, like any other medical procedure, is performed under circumstances that insure maximum safety for the patient. This interest obviously extends at least to the performing physician and his staff, to the facilities involved, to the availability of after-care, and to adequate provision for any complication or emergency that might arise. The prevalence of high mortality rates at illegal "abortion mills" strengthens, rather than weakens, the State's interest in regulating the conditions under which abortions are performed.

Medical procedures had been vastly improved since the late 1800s. Abortion during the early months of pregnancy was now safer than childbirth, suggesting a minimal need for state intervention. On the other hand, abortion during the last stages of pregnancy continued to involve serious risks and therefore regulation of procedures, facilities, and physician qualifications was more compelling.

With this understanding, the Court constructed a sliding scale for justifying state intervention. For maternal health and safety the state had compelling reasons to regulate abortion in the later stages of pregnancy. There were fewer compelling reasons in the early months. A similar sliding scale confronted the Court as it turned to the life-defining boundaries surrounding the embryo, fetus, or unborn child. The question became how to segment what was in truth a continuum.

Two polar positions for protecting life's boundaries were proposed by the lawyers arguing *Roe*: (1) no protections, with abortion on demand; (2) full protection for the unborn child from the moment of conception. The Court rejected both. Abortion is indeed a medical procedure, but so are appendectomies and root canals. More is at stake. The biological properties of the embryo, whatever your view of abortion, raise different questions about the protective boundaries of life than pulling a tooth or removing an appendix. The right to privacy was broad enough to include a mother's decision to terminate her pregnancy, but there were limits.[2]

With abortion on demand set aside, the Court turned to the protective boundaries of life and whether they were fully present at the moment, more accurately during the process, of conception and thus compelling of a decision prohibiting abortion. There was no crystal clear answer. The boundaries of protected life were hazy. The Court decided not to decide. "We need not resolve the difficult question of when life begins." The majority's decision noted. "When those trained in the respective disciplines of medicine, philosophy, and theology are unable to arrive at any consensus, the judiciary, at this point in the development of man's knowledge, is not in a position to speculate as to the answer."

Instead, the Court turned to the potential for life. In its contraception decisions, they had concluded that the potential for life inherent in the act of intercourse did not open the doorway for governmental intrusion. Conception, however, concretized the potential for life. Still there were ambiguities. There was evidence, the Court stated, "to indicate that conception is a 'process' over time, rather than an event." The argument anchoring life's protected boundaries on "potential" would be long lasting. Continuing advances in the understanding of conception, both inside and out of the womb, at the cellular and molecular levels, as a process rather than a moment, along with prenatal assessments of the potential quality-of-life, would provide grist for the mill among bio-ethicists, politicians, and legal scholars in the years ahead (see, for example, Iglesias 1984: 36; Reichlin 1997: 1–23; Singer 1993).

More settled was the idea that two sets of "fundamental rights" were involved—the health of the mother and the potential life she carried. There was a compelling state interest in limiting and protecting both. Where to draw the boundaries? The nine-month gestation period was divided into trimesters.

During the first trimester, when health risks of an abortion were low, even lower than carrying the pregnancy to term, there was no compelling reason for state intervention. On this basis, the attending physician, in consultation with the mother, should be free to determine, without interference from the state, whether the mother's pregnancy should be terminated. When it came to the potential life the mother was carrying, the point of compelling state interest came with "**viability**," the point at which the fetus was capable of "meaningful life outside the mother's womb." Given then available and rapidly improving medical technology, this probabilistic point was said to be somewhere between six and seven months after conception. After this point, state regulations designed to protect the interests of the unborn child could go so far as to prohibit abortion, except when necessary to preserve the "life or health" of the mother. With this reasoning in place, the *Roe* Court found the Texas abortion statute unconstitutional.

Still, the boundaries for the legitimate protection of life of both the mother and fetus remained hazy. The mother's health and life were taken into consideration.

---

2 In a bow to the eugenic past, the Court would justify limits on a woman's privacy by citing *Buck v. Bell*. The principle of *stare decisis* was alive and well.

Did this include mental as well as physical health? How threatening or debilitating did the threat to health have to be? These issues were more directly addressed in the companion case from Georgia, *Doe v. Bolton*. The protective boundaries were broadly drawn. Threats to the mother's health included, "all factors—physical, emotional, psychological, familial, and the woman's age—relevant to the well-being of the patient."

The boundaries for considering the health of the mother were wide. They even extended even to the family. Any remaining ambiguities were to be resolved by physicians. As Justice Blackmun wrote for the majority in *Doe* (when physicians were by in large still assumed to be men) "This allows the attending physician the room he needs to make his best medical judgment. And it is room that operates for the benefit, not the disadvantage, of the pregnant woman."

And so the stage was set. The shifting boundaries of protected life were divided into three-month increments determined by potential. For the fetus it was the increasing potential for a viable meaningful life, vaguely specified. For the mother it was the increasing potential threat to her health and life, broadly defined. The Supreme Court had been careful to "resolve the issue by constitutional measurement, free of emotion." They found in the penumbras of the Bill of Rights and the Fourteenth Amendment the right to privacy. They did not find full protections for prenatal life. Instead, they were persuaded that "the word 'person,' as used in the Fourteenth Amendment, does not include the unborn."

The Power of Empathy

This exclusionary conclusion, reached through the constraining influence of legal reasoning, would not be viewed with such steely-eyed detachment by a significant portion of the population. For many it became a clarion call for action. These now aroused advocates campaigned with increased energy. They pointed to ultrasound images of the unborn child to build empathy for its humanity. Poster-sized pictures of late-term abortions were carried to the streets to generate disgust at what the Supreme Court had wrought. They searched the penumbras of general principles, just as Supreme Court justices had done. This time the principles were found in scripture. Convinced that innocent lives were being taken, demonizing analogies were drawn with Nazi Germany. A small minority would hear direct messages from God and launch a violent and sometimes murderous campaign to protect life.

The power of images to generate empathy is nowhere more apparent than in the conversion of Dr. Bernard Nathanson. In his self-reflective book, *The Hand of God*, this former director of the largest abortion clinic in the United States wrote, "When ultrasound in the early 1970s confronted me with the sight of the embryo in a womb, I simply lost my faith in abortion on demand" (Nathanson 1996: 240). Dr. Nathanson's conversion had not been immediate. It evolved over a period of years, with early signs manifest in his November 1974 *New England Journal of Medicine* article, published just under two years after the *Roe and Doe* decisions. In this article, which reportedly turned out to be one of the most provocative in NEJM's publication history, Nathanson continued to support for abortion unregulated by law, but wrote with divided spirit and a "deeply troubled mind."

By the early 1980s, Nathanson had decided to work with a colleague and, with the aid of ultrasound technology, videotape what happened during an abortion of an 11- to 12-week-old fetus. He later recounted that in the editing studio the emotional impact of the visual images was so great that his colleague decided to abandon his abortion practice. Nathanson himself had stopped doing abortions five years earlier, but recalled that he was "shaken to the very roots of my soul" by what he saw. The empathetic human bonding generated by the visual images of the unborn was inescapable. Dr. Bernard Nathanson's conversion was complete.

Nathanson's still grainy videotape was shown during his subsequent lectures. Eventually, the videotape was edited further and made into a film, *The Silent Scream*. The explicit purpose was to generate empathy for the pain inflicted on the fetus during abortion and to underscore the human qualities of the developing fetus in the womb. It began with a voice overlay, "Now we can discern the chilling silent scream on the face of this child who is now facing imminent extinction."

This dramatic short introduction reflected the film's message. It was shown in the White House to President Reagan, who had recently published "Abortion and the Conscience of the Nation" (1983). The president provided members of Congress with a copy of the film. News accounts and editorials appeared and screenings were held in churches across the country.

For many, *The Silent Scream* was mind opening and conscience prodding. It was praised for raising public awareness of the evils of abortion much like Harriet Beecher Stowe's *Uncle Tom's Cabin* had done for slavery. It was also vilified as visually misleading and scientifically inaccurate (Dorfman et al. 2002). Accepted or not, the intended spoken and visual message of the film was clear. We were not dealing with a non-person outside communal boundaries of protection, as the Supreme Court had held. We were dealing instead with a human being, fully deserving of all the protections a moral community can offer.

This conclusion raised very troubling issues. Why would we even remotely tolerate what *The Silent Scream* claimed to be the tearing apart of a baby? Moderates advocating a pro-life position were willing to consider exceptions in cases of rape, incest, under-age pregnancies, and birth defects. Why? In what sense were the lives of these unborn children less worthy of protection?

Protests and Rescue Missions

Protests and disruptive actions escalated. Eventually, in a small, loosely connected, isolated, and tragically violent network, declared war against the "baby killers" in abortion clinics across the country. By 1979 a group of individuals had become disenchanted with what they saw as the timid, compromising position of some activists. Led by Paul and Judie Brown, they broke off and founded the American Life League (ALL). A short time later, in 1980, Joseph Scheidler, a former Benedictine monk widely considered the godfather of the early activist anti-abortion movement, organized the founding of the Pro-Life Action League (PLAL). For members of ALL and PLAL, there were no acceptable abortions. For these activists, abortion equaled murder. Thus framed, the call for confrontational politics among these now highly energized activists intensified.

The stated mission of the Pro-Life Action League was to save unborn children through "non-violent direct action." In pursuit of this mission, they published a manual, *Closed: 99 Ways to Stop Abortion*, at around the same time as the release of *The Silent Scream*. This how-to guide began with the sentence, "This book is based on the equation that abortion equals murder." It outlined a collection of methods for protesting and preventing abortion. The tactics were based on the premise that "No social movement in the history of this country has succeeded without activist(s) taking to the streets. Activism, including demonstrations, pickets, protests, and sit-ins, is necessary not only to save lives, but to garner public attention, bring the media into the struggle, and shake politicians into recognizing the determination of anti-abortion supporters" (Scheidler 1985: 17).

Joseph Scheidler and PLAL created a 40-minute film, *No Greater Joy*, depicting volunteers at work, carrying bibles, rosaries, and models of fetuses similar to those used in the *Silent Scream*. The objective of *No Greater Joy* was to mobilize resources by encouraging viewers to get involved. Viewers were told their counseling would be responsible for a baby being born and that this was a beautiful thing. They were cooperating with God in the most important fight on the face of the earth. The sidewalk counseling tactics shown were calm, supportive, and conversational. They did not always turn out that way. Eventually, the tape was updated with free access on the internet and accompanying advise on what to do "If somebody tells me to 'shut up' or to go away? (Prolife Action League N.D).

All tactics employed were not as calmly persuasive as those presented in *No Greater Joy*. Some were designed to obstruct, shock, and disgust. A subset of these were depicted in a second videotape, *Face the Truth,* also produced by PLAL (Prolife Action League, N.D.). The film began with a voice over, "*Face the Truth* is a bold new public education initiative that brings the reality of abortion to the highways and downtown intersections of cities and towns across America, confronting those who have turned away from the tragedy of our age." With protesting citizens, mothers and their children shown carrying greatly enlarged, dramatic and grotesque poster-sized photos of dismembered, aborted fetuses in the background, Scheidler's introductory statement was followed by another voice over, "America is in a death epic. We have killed 47 million children. That's unconscionable and something has to be done, and we are doing what has to be done. We are showing America the face of abortion."

The strong framing message was straightforward: Life is sacred and should be protected. Life begins at conception. Existing laws are illegitimate, unjust, and immoral. As one icon of the anti-abortion movement put it, "The bottom line is that at a certain point there is not only the right, but the duty, to disobey the State" (Schaeffer 1981: 120). This argument was securing a broader public, reflective of a national network of aroused organizations and individuals (Blanchard 1994). Energized by motivating disgust, empathy, and how-to recipes for action, these organizations and individuals expanded their moral crusade.

Violence Increases

Following the rise in clinic arson and bombings in the late 1970s, there was a drop-off in violence directed at abortion clinics and staff. In 1984–1985, the years *The Silent Scream* and *Closed: 99 Ways to Stop Abortion* were released, things changed. On Christmas Day, 1984, three clinics were bombed by a small group of young activists associated with a local Assembly of God church in Pensacola, Florida. They identified with the Old Testament story of Gideon, the slayer of those who offered infant sacrifices to Baal, referring to their protest efforts as the Gideon Project (Blanchard and Prewitt 1993). One of the suspects, soon arrested, claimed his actions had been "a birthday gift for Jesus." It turned out that one motivating factor had been the showing of graphic images and films at his church. They had left a "strong impression."

These young activists were only loosely connected with PLAL and Joseph Scheidler, but Scheidler along with other national anti-abortion figures attended the trial and spoke favorably of their activities in the media. The Gideon Project was not an isolated incident. Between 1984 and 1985 the number of bombings and arson incidents at abortion clinics, as reported by the National Abortion Federation, rose dramatically to 52, more than quadrupling the previous high water mark between 1977 and 1978. An additional 107 bomb threats were recorded. Death threats also peaked at 45. These threats included one directed at Supreme Court Justice Harry Blackmun, who had written the *Roe* decision. It came from a militant anti-abortion organization, which was implicated in the kidnapping of an abortion doctor and his wife in Illinois. The threat against Justice Blackmun was received in October at about time an anti-abortion activist had disrupted the highly regimented atmosphere of Supreme Court hearings. A few months later, in February 1985, a bullet passed through the window of

Justice Blackmun's home. No one was injured, but this incident marked the first time a Supreme Court justice had been the victim in a shooting investigation.

The increasingly aggressive militancy, now violent, did not go unnoticed. Criminal charges were lodged, arrests made, lawsuits filed, and counter demonstrations planned. Among moderates, disillusionment and a sense of betrayal set in. As one angry advocate of non-violent, pro-life strategies put it, "The work we're doing, it totally shoots it down. There are a lot of minds and hearts to win over. Blowing up clinics only hardens hearts" (Risen and Thomas 1998: 94). Less moderate anti-abortion religious groups joined forces, organized additional clinic blockades, and gave birth to new organizations.

Operation Rescue

In the early years of anti-abortion efforts, the Catholic Church had been the dominant force. When protestant fundamentalists joined the cause, motivated by Francis Schaeffer's *A Christian Manifesto,* they moved center stage. One adherent, a young charismatic Pentecostal minister Randall Terry, still in his twenties, had become closely aligned with the efforts of PLAL and Joseph Scheidler. In 1986, with their relationship strained over how aggressive the anti-abortion forces should be, Terry joined others in the formation of Operation Rescue.

At the time, Scheidler was facing a series of lawsuits, and there is some indication that Operation Rescue emerged at least in part to avoid legal battles being launched against Scheidler and PLAL. Whatever its genesis, Operation Rescue was far more confrontational. It took seriously and applied to abortion the admonitions of Proverbs 24:11 "Deliver those who are being taken away to death, and those who are staggering to slaughter." Within Operation Rescue, sidewalk counseling, and other comparatively modest protests gave way to massive demonstrations and blockades.

Organized and led by Randall Terry, the first major Operation Rescue clinic blockade took place in 1987, in Cherry Hill, New Jersey. A sympathetic reporter covered the event, "Over 200 people were arrested ... in the nation's largest 'rescue mission' for unborn children, conducted at the Cherry Hill Women's Center in Cherry Hill, New Jersey. The protestors, who flew in from 19 different states at their own expense, came to the clinic to be trained in the civil disobedience tactic of barring pregnant women from abortion facilities in order to save the lives of unborn babies" (*Foreunner* 1987). A subsequent assessment suggested the activities in Cherry Hill were transformative, "Clinic sit-ins and blockades were no longer small, isolated local events; they had suddenly become the most important form of political expression in the entire national debate over abortion" (Risen and Thomas 1998: 263).

It was not until the next year, however, at the 1988 Democratic National Convention in Atlanta, Georgia, that Operation Rescue came to prominent national attention.

A large protest was organized, and again several hundred arrests ensued. Terry was interviewed shortly after the demonstrations (*Forerunner* 1998). Just as Supreme Court Justices had found justification for the right to privacy in the penumbras of the U.S. Constitution, Terry found justification for his activities in his interpretation of scriptures.

INTERVIEWER: What is the philosophy behind Operation Rescue?

TERRY: The foundation of Operation Rescue is a call to people and the Church to repent. The Church has sinned before God by allowing children to be ripped apart and mothers to be exploited. We have sat idly by and have done virtually nothing.

INTERVIEWER: How do you justify violating the law in your fight against abortion?

TERRY: Easily. When God's law and man's law conflict, Scripture clearly teaches that man is not to obey that law. Some examples are when the three Hebrew children were thrown into the fire, when the apostles were jailed for preaching the Gospel, and when the stone was rolled away from the Lord's tomb. That was in defiance of a man-made law. God never gave the government a blank check to do what it wants to do. It is a heresy to teach Christians to obey a law which runs counter to His law.

Roe Reexamined

As the 1980s drew to a close, by most accounts, the 7–2 majority in the *Roe* and *Doe* cases had become something closer to five–four. In 1989 this shifting mixture of proclivities among Supreme Court justices became evident in a case emerging from a recently passed Missouri statute, Webster v. Reproductive Health Services.

Several aspects of the law were at issue, including its definition of when life started, but the major magnet for controversy was the determination of "viability" and the utility of the trimester structure. While the Court did not overturn *Roe*, it was close. There was no clear majority, only pluralities for differing versions of the court's findings. Chief Justice Rehnquist, joined by two of his colleagues, Justices White and Kennedy, concluded, "Roe's rigid trimester analysis has proved to be unsound in principle and unworkable in practice … the Roe trimester framework should be abandoned." An even harsher assessment was provided by Justice Scalia, "It thus appears that the mansion of constitutionalized abortion law, constructed overnight in *Roe v. Wade*, must be disassembled doorjamb by doorjamb, and never entirely brought down, no matter how wrong it may be."

As much dissention as there was on the Court in *Webster*, *Roe* was not overturned. Nevertheless, the door was opened ever so slightly. Legislators in Pennsylvania entered. For anti-abortion advocates, knowing that presidents Reagan and Bush had now appointed the majority of the Court, the Pennsylvania statute offered a ray of hope. The law was challenged. Critics of *Roe* were disappointed. Justice O'Connor, in *Planned Parenthood v. Casey* (1992) wrote for the majority, "We are led to conclude this: the essential holding of *Roe v. Wade* should be retained and once again reaffirmed." This affirmation of *Roe* came on the heels of heightened clinic blockades. One of national significance took place in Wichita, Kansas. It would eventually play out almost twenty years later in the shooting death of a local abortion provider.

The Summer of Mercy

By the early 1990s, Operation Rescue's confrontational tactics and organizing influence, focused on three abortion clinics in Wichita, Kansas, in what came to be known as the Summer of Mercy. They gave special attention to a clinic run by Dr. George Tiller. Tiller was advertising nationally his services to provide elective abortions in the second and third trimesters. Entrances to Tiller's and two other Wichita clinics were blocked. Police were called out. Somewhere between 2,500 and 3,000 arrests were made, mainly for minor offenses such as trespassing. A federal judge issued decrees, based on post-Civil War legislation designed to limit intimidation and deprivation of civil rights (Ku Klux Klan Act of 1871).

When local police were not cooperative, the judge asked federal marshals to enforce his decrees. President Bush countermanded the judge's orders. After almost seven weeks of protest, orders, counter orders, and substantial national publicity, some 25,000 to 35,000 persons (estimates varied) gathered in Wichita State University's stadium in late August. The state's governor, the city's mayor, and several high profile anti-abortion activists including leaders of organizations such as the recently disbanded Moral Majority and the recently established Christian Coalition joined them. The aim was to underscore their common cause and celebrate their commitment to the "Hope for the Heartland." These citizens and organizations were a political force to be reckoned with (see http://www.dr-tiller.com/mercy.htm).

Dr. George Tiller became "Tiller the Baby Killer." Persons who favored the right to choose were characterized as murderers. Persons adamantly opposed to abortion under any circumstances were painted as narrow-minded religious fanatics. Following the Summer of Mercy, similar events were organized elsewhere, though they did not attract nearly as much attention. Counteracting lawsuits continued. In 1992, prompted by events in Wichita and similar protests in other cities, the bipartisan Freedom of Access to Clinic Entrances (FACE) Act was filed in the U.S. Congress.

While this bill was being debated, a case examining the applicability of the Ku Klux Act of 1871 for regulating clinic blockades, used by the federal judge in Wichita, had reached the Supreme Court for a second hearing. Justice department attorney, John Roberts Jr., who in 2005 would become the 17th Chief Justice of the Supreme

Court, argued the case for the Bush administration, suggesting that the federal judge in Wichita had been wrong.

Since actions of protestors were even-handed, Roberts argued, attempts to prevent abortion were not discriminatory. Resolution of the issue should be left to state legislative bodies and courts. Lawyers for NOW and women's health clinics disagreed. They saw a nationwide and systematic conspiracy to intimidate abortion providers and to prevent women from exercising their civil rights. Limiting such discriminatory actions was precisely what the drafters of the 1871 Act had in mind. The Supreme Court, in another split vote, sided with attorney Roberts and the Justice Department (*Jayne Bray, et al., Petitioners v. Alexandria Women's Health Clinic et al.* 1993). Abortion clinics and their clients would have to look elsewhere for protection.

Taking Lives to Save Lives

Two months later, on March 10, 1993, shortly after the 20th anniversary of *Roe*, Dr. David Gunn, who provided services in clinics in Alabama, Georgia, and Florida, became the first abortion provider to be murdered by anti-abortion extremists. Gunn had been targeted after his picture, phone number, and address appeared on a "Wanted" poster created by Operation Rescue and distributed at an Alabama rally held in support of Randall Terry (Booth 1993). Confronted outside his Pensacola, Florida, office by protesters carrying posters reading "David Gunn Kills Babies," Dr. Gunn was shot three times as he got out of his car on a Wednesday morning by a man dressed in a gray suit shouting, "Don't kill any more babies." The previous Sunday this same man, it turned out, had asked his congregation to pray for Dr. Gunn's soul and conversion.

The assailant was Michael Griffin. He had grown up in Pensacola. Similar to participants in The Gideon Project, he was an active member of a local Assembly of God church. He had been influenced by what his attorneys characterized as the relentless rhetoric and graphic images shown to him by his preacher, a local anti-abortion extremist and former KKK member (Rother 1994).

The minister was the regional director of Rescue America, an organization evolved from Operation Rescue. He had been instrumental in leading the protest outside the clinic where Dr. Gunn was shot. Shortly after Dr. Gunn's murder, the minister was quoted as saying in apparent reference to federal legislation, "There's talk of making protesting abortion clinics a felony. If you start talking about that, people are just going to find other ways of dealing with it" (Booth 1993: A01).

A few months after the shooting death of Dr. Gunn, Dr. George Tiller, the major focus of the Summer of Mercy demonstrations, was wounded in a botched attempt on his life as he was leaving work one evening. Shelley Shannon, the admitted assailant and a participant in the Summer of Mercy, was a sympathizer with Michael Griffin.

She, too, had become convinced that more drastic action was called for. Shannon's intensified convictions along with her destructive and violent actions directed at other clinics largely on the west coast are documented in court records as well as her diary and letters sent to family and friends. Like others, she turned to her God's word and prayer for support.

Of Michael Griffin, she wrote in her diary,

> He didn't shoot Mother Teresa, he shot a mass murderer such as Saddam Hussien (*sic*) or Hitler. I don't even think it is accurately termed 'murder'. God is the only one who knows whether Gunn would ever have repented or if he would have killed another 5,000 babies and probably 3 or 4 more women, who probably weren't Christians either, and then died with even more to condemn him … I am not convinced that God didn't require it of Michael to do this. It is possible. I am praying God will push more of us 'off the deep end.'

In this same diary entry, she continued,

> I am glad for those who are publicly refusing to condemn Michael Griffin. I'm sure there will be more of these works. Mine is clear. This morning in bed it seemed God asked, "Is there any doubt?" … Again He asked, "Is there any doubt?" I could recognize some fear and other things. The third time He asked, "Is there any doubt?" No, Lord. Please help me do it right.

A short time later, referencing a verse from Isaiah 6:8 ("Then I heard the voice of the Lord saying, 'Whom shall I send? And who will go for us?' And I said, 'Here am I. Send me!'"), Shelley Shannon took a bus from Grants Pass, Oregon, to Oklahoma City, rented a car at the airport, drove some 160 miles north to Wichita, Kansas, and "went off the deep end" to become one of those messengers of God she was praying for. She later wrote from jail to her daughter about first going into the clinic and then back outside to wait until Dr. Tiller and a woman employee left work that evening,

> I dressed up and fixed my hair different and went inside (had a gun in a purse) and got a look around, but couldn't find Tiller. [She left the clinic and waited outside until persons, including Dr. Tiller emerged.] I ran up [To Tiller's car] and shot through the window, I think 6 times. I turned around and aimed at the lady, but I didn't shoot. It seemed like God (or an angel?) said, "Run for your life Shelley!" So I ran. Ran through a little creek spot & up to where the car was…. Tried not to look suspicious…. Got in, and drove off.

At trial, it would be revealed that Rachelle Ranae "Shelley" Shannon had been leading a double life for some time. For many of her friends, as reported shortly thereafter, hearing that she was involved in this shooting, and, as it was soon revealed, arson, bombings and vandalism at several other clinics, was like hearing that "Minnie Mouse had bombed the White House."

The shootings of doctors Gunn and Tiller drew substantial public attention and concern. The Freedom of Access to Clinic Entrances legislation had failed to pass Congress in 1992. Following the murder of Dr. Gunn and the shooting of Dr. Tiller in 1993, the bill was reintroduced and supported by a bipartisan coalition of senators and representatives, including presidential candidate and Kansas Senator Bob Dole. This time it passed. The House approved the bill on May 5, 1994. One week later the Senate agreed. A good deal of testimony and relevant data had been gathered. Between 1977 and 1993 more than 1,000 acts of violence against providers of reproductive health services had been reported. In addition to the murder of Dr. David Gunn, there had been at least 36 bombings, 81 arsons, 131 death threats, 84 assaults, 2 kidnappings, 327 clinic invasions, 71 chemical attacks, and more than 6,000 blockades and related disruptions of reproductive health clinics.

On May 26, 1994, President Clinton signed the FACE legislation into law. While the Supreme Court had found the Ku Klux Klan Act of 1871 inapplicable, FACE provided the sought after protections for those seeking abortions and those providing services by making it a federal crime to use force, the threat of force, or physical obstruction to injure, intimidate, or interfere with persons obtaining or providing reproductive health services. Reported incidents of clinic protest activities, as recorded by the National Abortion Federation, tapered off. The number of blockades had been 83 and 66 in 1992 and 1993, respectively. In 1994 there were 25 and in 1995 the total was 5. The number of attendant arrests and reported instances of vandalism likewise dropped. There would be an increase in picketing and peaks of more threatening activity in later years, such as the increase of anthrax threats in 2001, but there was a sense among supporters and opponents alike that the FACE Act was having an impact.

Still, there were problems. Four additional murders and eight attempted murders occurred in 1994. These murders, justified by extremists, were condemned, in varying degrees, by high profile religious organizations such as the Southern Baptist Convention, and activists such as Bernard Nathanson, John Cardinal O'Connor, Ann Scheidler, and Gary North (The Nashville Statement of Conscience 1994; North 1994). For these individuals and organizations taking life to protect life did not make sense. Others disagreed. Their efforts would continue.

The Army of God

For a small, highly motivated minority commitment to lethal action continued. For these individuals the time had come for a violent response to the killing of children. They had waited long enough, perhaps too long. The injustice and illegitimacy of existing laws were clear. They were witnessing a holocaust, and they were no longer going to stand idly by. Parallels with the Nazis and the abolition of slavery and the violent anti-slavery actions of John Brown were repeatedly invoked. Biblical scriptures were used to justify and frame their actions, and to demonize abortion providers. One such group called themselves The Army of God.

Shelley Shannon's letters and diary, along with her testimony and evidence presented at her trial shed important light on how violence was spreading in contagion-like fashion among a small, isolated and loosely connected group of extreme adherents to the anti-abortion cause. In particular, the Army of God's manual, dug up in Shannon's back yard following her arrest, brought increased and unintended attention to this shadowy organization. The Army's loose-knit structure was evident in the manual where it was claimed the Army of God was real, but members rarely "… communicate with one another. Very few have ever met each other. And when they do, each is usually unaware of the other's soldier status. That is why the Feds will never stop this Army. Never. And we have not yet even begun to fight." (Army of God Manual)

The history of this organization remains clouded, but folklore indicates the original version of the Manual was drafted by some of the jailed Operation Rescue protesters at the 1988 Democratic Convention. In a later edition of the manual, the religious footing for their violent response to increased federal regulations was starkly stated in an explicit warning:

> We, the remnant of God-fearing men and women of the United States of Amerika, do officially declare war on the entire child killing industry … Our life for yours— simple equation. Dreadful. Sad. Reality, nonetheless. You shall not be tortured at our hands. Vengeance belongs to God only. However, execution is rarely gentile (*sic*).

Reflecting these same sentiments, Neal Horsley, a central figure in the Army of God,[3] wrote a piece, "Understanding the Army of God," shortly after a clinic bombing in Birmingham, Alabama, for which Eric Rudolph was eventually convicted, and where an off-duty policeman was killed and a woman seriously injured.

> If all the previous evidence did not make it clear, the bomb in the Birmingham clinic should prove to all that the Army of God has entered this warfare…. Do not expect this war to end until legalized abortion is repealed. The Army of God is an evanescent, amorphous, autonomous and spontaneous eruption of individuals…. People enraged by the war being waged in this nation against God's children will continue to engage in terrorist actions. Because the government of the USA has

---

3 HBO's 2000 America Under Cover documentary, *Soldiers in the Army of God*, featured Horsley, along with Paul Hill, Bob Lokey, and Michael Bray.

become a godless and apostate body, the people who rise up in arms against such idolatry deserve the name "The Army of God."[4]

The sense of injustice was deep. Legitimacy for the government was withdrawn. Those involved in the baby killing industry had hardened their blackened, jaded hearts. A demonizing sense of Us and Them was complete. Violence followed. This destructive and lethal violence would be systematically advocated by fellow travelers in the Army of God, including its Chaplain, Michael Bray, who wrote, *A Time to Kill*, wherein he argued it was justifiable to kill abortion doctors. Similarly, Eric Rudolph wrote,

> I am not an anarchist. I have nothing against government or law enforcement in general. It is solely for the reason that this government has legalized the murder of children that I have no allegiance to nor do I recognize the legitimacy of this particular government in Washington.... Because I believe that abortion is murder, I also believe that force is justified in an attempt to stop it.[5]

It was a former Presbyterian minister, Paul Hill, however, who provided the most extensive exposition of the position taken by this loosely connected group of self-acknowledged terrorists. Following several days of protesting, in late July, 1994, Hill shot and killed Dr. John Britton, along with his armed escort, seriously wounding the escort's wife in the process. Dr. Britton had been recruited to Pensacola, in part to replace the services of Dr. Gunn. Hill, who admitted the killings, was convicted and sentenced to death. While awaiting execution, he brought together and expanded his writings in a manuscript, *Mix My Blood With the Blood of the Unborn*.

---

4 This piece was later revised and posted on his website, www.christiangallery.com.

   In his introduction to the revised article, Horsley writes: "I originally wrote this article in the immediate aftermath of a Birmingham abortion clinic bombing in 1997 when someone—Eric Rudolph?—sent a note saying the Army of God had planted the bomb. Post 9/11/2001, the only thing I add to what I wrote before is to point out that Muslim terrorists call themselves the Army of God just as this abortion clinic bomber did. It is most remarkable that President George W. Bush has finally acknowledged and admitted and declared the war that had gone undeclared in this nation ever since 1973 when the government of the USA in *Roe. v. Wade* effectively declared war against the children of God. If you want to understand the Army of God in the USA, read the article entitled "Exploding the Myth of the Army of God."

5 Rudolph had become widely known after hiding in the woods of North Carolina for some five years before being captured and facing four trials in four separate jurisdictions for his violent activities. See http://www.armyofgod.com/EricRudolphHomepage.html.

Hill was executed before he was able to finish his book. In the week just prior to his execution, Hill and his supporters decided that the manuscript would be published in its unedited condition. Subsequently, one of Hill's friends and confidants, Rev. Donald Spitz, then Director of Pro-life Virginia, put the unedited manuscript online (Spitz N.D.). The grounding principle was succinctly stated: "It is certain that the innocent should be defended with the means necessary, and since the unborn are innocent, it is equally certain that they should be defended with the means necessary."

Two weeks after Paul Hill had killed Dr. Britton and his escort in Pensacola, Florida, a *Time* article appeared, asking the question, "Why Not Kill the Baby Killers." This short piece began and ended with a nod to Hill's logic.

> The logic of Paul Hill—that abortion equals baby killing, that there is a "holocaust" going on and that therefore killing an abortionist is "justifiable homicide"—may be insane, but it is more consistent than the logic of those who share all of Hill's premises but reject his conclusion....
>
> Even someone who believes that abortion is murder might reasonably conclude that killing abortionists is not justified because America is not Nazi Germany: we are a democracy under the rule of law. But once a group accepts the premise that the laws enacted by a democratic society are no legitimate deterrent in efforts to prevent "baby killing," it becomes harder to see what is wrong with stopping the murders by killing the murderers. The Operation Rescue people are not pacifists. They do not believe in the principle that violence is always wrong, even in response to violence. So why not kill the doctors? Paul Hill understands their logic better than they do.
>
> (Kinsley 1994)

On September 3, 2003, Paul Hill became the first person executed for killings associated with abortion clinics. His last recorded words were an appeal to the Golden Rule, "Two of the last things I'd like to say, if you believe abortion is a lethal force, you should oppose the force and do what you have to do to stop it. May God help you to protect the unborn as you would want to be protected" (Office of the Clark County Prosecuting Attorney N.D.). Other clinics were bombed and doctors performing abortions killed and assaulted,[6] but with Paul Hill's execution we came full circle. This former Presbyterian minister, calling on a higher law, justified killing those he charged with killing babies. He in turn was executed. Both life-ending actions were justified by

---

6 In addition to Drs. John Britton and David Gunn, in 1994 two receptionists were killed in Massachusetts and Virginia. In 1998 a security guard at a clinic was killed in Alabama. In this same year in Dr. Barnett Slepian was shot to death in his home in New York. In addition, as reported by the National Abortion Federation, there were numerous attempted murders and assaults during this same time period.

invoking the imperative, "Life is sacred and should be protected." They differed only in how they defined the protective boundaries of life, their sense of injustice, and the legitimacy given to the actions taken.

Some six years later, on May 31, 2009, the story continued. Dr. George Tiller, who had escaped Shelley Shannon's attempted murder, was shot to death while attending church. His assailant used the defense of justified homicide. Following Dr. Tiller's murder, Randall Terry released a statement:

> George Tiller was a mass-murderer. We grieve for him that he did not have time to properly prepare his soul to face God. I am more concerned that the Obama Administration will use Tiller's killing to intimidate pro-lifers into surrendering our most effective rhetoric and actions. Abortion is still murder. And we still must call abortion by its proper name; murder.
>
> Those men and women who slaughter the unborn are murderers according to the Law of God. We must continue to expose them in our communities and peacefully protest them at their offices and homes, and yes, even their churches.
>
> (Veritas N.D.)

More direct justifications for Tiller's murder instantly appeared on outlets for the Army of God, one titled "A Just End to a Violent, Wicked Man" (The Army of God N.D.).

Dr. Tiller was best known, revered, and reviled for his willingness to provide late term therapeutic abortions, when the fetus was, as some would note, mere inches from life.

DISCUSSION QUESTIONS

1. What role has the U.S. Supreme Court played in determining reproductive rights? Do you believe that it has overstepped its boundaries? Why or why not?
2. How have advances in medical technologies affected the abortion debate?
3. The concepts of "trimesters" and "viability" have had significant impact on how we understand pregnancy in the United States. Describe these concepts and how they have affected the reproductive rights debate.
4. How have improvements in medical technology affected our ability to empathize with the unborn?
5. Should right-to-life activists be able to protest outside of reproductive clinics? What restrictions, if any, should be placed on their activities?
6. How have some members of the right-to-life movement used religion and scripture to condone or justify the use violence against abortion providers?

IV: Inches from Life

⧽⧼

Dr. George Tiller had been labeled "Tiller the Baby Killer" by those opposed to his late-term abortion practice. Those who condemned him were convinced they were doing God's will even if it meant taking life to protect life. While extreme, such activists were embedded in a national social movement. A high water mark was the 1991 Summer of Mercy.

A local federal judge had issued an injunction to end the clinic blockades in Wichita, Kansas. His orders were backed by the use of federal marshals. The President of the United States, sympathetic to the demonstrators, had countermanded the judge's action. Lawsuits were filed to resolve the issues. One involved a young Justice Department attorney in his late thirties, John Roberts, who argued before the Supreme Court on behalf of Jayne Bray and her husband, Michael Bray, who had authored the anti-abortion book, *A Time to Kill: A Study Concerning the Use of Force and Abortion* (*Jayne Bray, et al., Petitioners v. Alexandria Women's Health Clinic, et al.* 1993).

A little over a decade later, in 2005, attorney Roberts would become Chief Justice of the Supreme Court. In 2007 he joined four of his colleagues in a decision that upheld the Partial-Birth Abortion Ban Act of 2003, signed into law by President George W. Bush (*Gonzales, Attorney General v. Carhart, et al.* 2007). This Act outlawed a subset of late-term abortion procedures that had so troubled and outraged those opposed to Dr. Tiller's practice (The Partial-Birth Abortion Ban Act). The years between the 1991 Summer of Mercy and the Supreme Court's 2007 validation of the federal law banning specific late-term abortion procedures were eventful. The major findings of *Roe* and *Doe* were solidified. The boundary where abortion became infanticide was clarified. It was inches from birth.

Words and Images

The applicability of moral principles and the perceived legitimacy of law depend how issues are framed; on the analogies drawn, the meaning assigned to words, and the emotional impact of images. During the 1990s phrases evolved, acronyms were employed, and illustrations produced, all to frame the moral meaning of ending a pregnancy at the very edge of where, all agreed, life is present.

One such phrase was "partial-birth abortion." It was not a medical phrase. It was a phrase of political art, crafted by social activists and politicians. It evolved from a description of a newly developed medical procedure outlined by Dr. W. Martin Haskell at a national abortion risk management seminar held in Dallas in September 1992 (Haskell 1992). Dr. Haskell was the physician-owner of a women's center in Cincinnati, Ohio. He had performed over 700 abortions using what he called Dilation and Extraction (D&X) procedures. These procedures were easier and safer than the more commonly used dilation and evacuation (D&E) methods. He wanted to let his colleagues know how it was done.

Dr. Haskell was no activist and had not been threatened directly by persons such as Michael Griffin or Paul Hill, but his practice precisely illustrated what so troubled the organizers of the Summer of Mercy. When talking with his colleagues at the abortion risk management seminar, however, these organizers were not what Dr. Haskell had in mind. He was interested instead in reducing the medical risks in late second-trimester and early third-trimester abortions, offering details on a safe, quick outpatient procedure he had developed.

Haskell's detailed description for the benefit of his colleagues was laced with technical descriptors. These were of little interest to those who stood in opposition. Other portions of Haskell's presentation did, however, catch their attention. Perhaps unwittingly, Dr. Haskell, when describing the technical details, also highlighted the humanity of the fetus and thereby generated empathy for the infant, and repulsion for the actions being described.

> The surgeon introduces a large grasping forceps … When the instrument appears on the sonogram screen, the surgeon is able to open and close its jaws to firmly and reliably grasp a lower extremity … and pulls the extremity into the vagina.…
>
> The skull lodges at the internal cervical (opening). Usually there is not enough dilation for it to pass through. The fetus is oriented … spine up … the surgeon takes a pair of blunt curved Metzenbaum scissors in the right hand. He carefully advances the tip, curved down, along the spine and under his middle finger until he feels it contact the base of the skull under the tip of his middle finger.… the surgeon then forces the scissors into the base of the skull.… Having safely entered the skull, he spreads the scissors to enlarge the opening.
>
> The surgeon removes the scissors and introduces a suction catheter into this hole and evacuates the skull contents. With the catheter still in place, he applies traction to the fetus, removing it completely from the patient.

In an interview a year following his presentation, Haskell was asked, "Does it bother you that a second trimester fetus so closely resembles a baby?" "I really don't think about it." He responded. "Sure it becomes more physically developed but it lacks emotional development. It doesn't have the mental capacity for self-awareness. It's never been an ethical dilemma for me." Later in the same interview he was asked, "Does the fetus feel pain?" Admitting some ignorance, he again drew the humanizing line at self-awareness, likening the fetus to a pet. "I'm not an expert, but my understanding is that fetal development is insufficient for consciousness. It's a lot like pets. We like to think they think like we do. We ascribe human-like feelings to them, but they are not capable of the same self-awareness we are. It's the same with fetuses" ("2nd Trimester Abortion" 1993: 18).

For physicians, the procedures described might have been clinically straightforward and helpful. For others, they were a jarring offense against life. Anti-abortion activists did not miss the humanizing implications. Starting with Bernard Nathanson's film, *The Silent Scream*, anti-abortion advocates had attempted to frame the abortion debate through graphic images and rhetoric, picturing the fetus in the sanctuary of the womb as a small, delicate, vulnerable person deserving of, in every way, our full respect and protection. During the early stages of pregnancy depicted in Nathanson's film, these images and conclusions were ambiguous. The ultra sound images were grainy and hard to decipher. The fetal models used in the film were not always to scale. Claims of early-term fetal suffering could be and were questioned.

More dramatic were the words of Dr. Haskell. Anti-abortion advocates had been handed a gift. Unwittingly, a doctor, well experienced with abortions, was making their case for them. D&X abortions involved the intentional killing of a partially born human being, in many cases occurring beyond the point of *viability* of 24 to 28 weeks, alluded to in *Roe*. Unlike first trimester abortions, the late-term fetus took on easily identified human qualities and was clearly capable of experiencing pain.

This became evident in testimony a later congressional hearing offered by a self-described pro-choice nurse, attending the D&X abortion of a 26½-week fetus. "The baby's little fingers were clasping and unclasping, and his feet were kicking. Then the doctor stuck the scissors through the back of his head, and the baby's arms jerked out in a flinch, a startle reaction, like a baby does when he thinks that he might fall. The doctor opened up the scissors, stuck a high-powered suction tube into the opening and sucked the baby's brains out. Now the baby was completely limp. I was really completely unprepared for what I was seeing. I almost threw up as I watched the doctor do these things" (Testimony of Brenda Pratt Shafer, Subcommittee on the Constitution, U.S. House of Representatives 1996). Actions taken during late-term abortions might be described as dilation and extraction, or D&X, for clinicians. For others, they were the destruction of a small, vulnerable human being. The procedures were a repulsive abomination.

The National Right to Life Committee (NRLC) was the first to take up the charge on a national scale. They were aware, as flawed as its message was, that *The Silent Scream* had been an effective call to action. Its title drew attention; even its grainy ultrasound images and illustrative not-always-to-scale fetal models generated empathy, commitment, and action. Using Dr. Haskell's description of his procedures, they aimed to do the same thing.

Images, originally easily reproducible cartoon-like sketches drawn by an Oregon activist, Jenny Westberg (Gorney 2004), and later refined into color representations for the Internet, were produced and disseminated ("Partial Birth Abortion" N.D.). They depicted Dr. Haskell's description of D&X procedures. Their message was clear. The life of a small, vulnerable baby was at risk; the last picture showing the instant when the suction catheter was placed in the infant's skull.

Westberg's early images drew the attention of Keri Harrison, who would draft the 1995 Partial-Birth Abortion Ban legislation, carried by a Florida Congressman, Charles Canady; legislation eventually vetoed by President Clinton. For Harrison it was simple. "To think that a human being would actually hold a little baby in his or her hand, and then kill it—that's what got me. If you're holding that child in your hand, and knowingly killing the child, you can't argue any more that it's not really a human being. You just can't do it" (Gorney 2004).

A dramatic phrase was needed to capture the procedure, a phrase that would be accurate and compelling, but not a phrase that would connect their efforts with the alienating fringe elements of the anti-abortion movement. "Late-term abortion" was too ambiguous and encompassing. It also left the sense that the procedure was fully covered by the *Roe* and *Doe* decisions. In D&X procedures the fetus was moved into the birth canal. It was in many ways similar to a premature birth. If the cervix dilated a bit more, the child would emerge through the birth canal without assistance. All this was visually apparent from the Westberg drawings. Harrison would later recall, that while throwing around terms with Representative Canady and NRLC lobbyist, Douglas Johnson, "We called it the most descriptive thing we could call it" (Gorney 2004). The fetus was indeed just inches from birth. "Partial-birth abortion" was decided upon as the phrase to frame their message.

Protecting Health as Well as Life

A bill, the Partial-Birth Abortion Ban Act of 1995, was drafted. It passed the Congress in December, but not enough to override a presidential veto (i.e., House of Representatives: 288–139; Senate: 54–44).

When explaining his veto, President Clinton did not refer to "partial-birth" abortions, but rather that he had "long opposed late-term abortions except where necessary to protect the life or health of the mother." Threats to the mother's life had been included. "Health" had been left out. Had the bill included an exception for "serious health consequences," consequences including "serious physical harm, often including losing the ability to have more children," President Clinton would have signed it. Indeed, he noted, "I would sign it now."

Concluding his remarks, the president wanted everyone to know he understood and agreed with "the desire to eliminate the use of a procedure that appears inhumane. But to eliminate it without taking into consideration the rare and tragic circumstances in which its use may be necessary would be even more inhumane." Both Congress and President Clinton wanted to protect life and alleviate suffering. They disagreed on where the boundaries should be drawn and how competing values should be resolved.

Why had supporters of the bill not included a "health" exception? Why were others so adamant that this be done? Those opposing the "health" exception recalled the language of *Roe's* companion case, *Doe v. Bolton*, wherein the Court had defined health broadly to include, "all factors—physical, emotional, psychological, familial, and the woman's age—relevant to the well-being of the patient." This was no boundary at all. Anyone could conceivably claim a "health" exception. Opening the door to the health exception would be opening the floodgates to the disregard for life. It would mean partial-birth abortions on demand.

Advocates for the health exception, by contrast, focused on circumstances when suffering and damage to life's chances were severe. Some fetuses, if born, would have debilitating deformities or severe brain damage, sometimes detected late in the pregnancy. A meaningful life for the yet to be born infant was precluded. In many cases letting the child be born and fighting for its ultimately unattainable survival meant a severe strain on the financial and emotional resources of the family. In some, albeit rare cases, not allowing late-term abortions represented a threat to the health and physical well-being of the mother, including her ability to have children in the future. The mechanisms of the law, useful for general policy, but ham-handed in individual cases, should not intrude. These difficult, often tragic decisions should be left to persons most directly involved.

President Clinton's veto was issued on April 10, 1996. Those committed to respecting the autonomy of mothers, families and their physicians to make these intensely personal decisions were relieved. Those concerned with what they saw as the taking of life just inches from birth and an emerging culture deemphasizing the sanctity of life were incensed. They did not plan to let the issue drop.

In an impassioned speech, urging his colleagues to override President Clinton's veto, Representative Henry Hyde foresaw profound society-wide consequences. "It is not just the babies that are dying for the lethal sin of being unwanted or being handicapped or malformed. We are dying, and not from the darkness, but from the cold, the coldness of self-brutalization that chills our sensibilities, deadens our conscience and allows us to think of this unspeakable act as an act of compassion."(Hyde, 1996)

Henry Hyde was not alone. A week after his veto, President Clinton received a letter of protest from the National Conference of Catholic Bishops. With "deep sorrow and dismay" those signing the letter found the president's veto "beyond comprehension for those who hold human life sacred." These religious leaders were convinced the president's action would ensure "the continued use of the most heinous act to kill a tiny infant just seconds from taking his or her first breath outside the womb."

They found the President's assessment of "health" too broad, noting, "If a woman is 'too young' or 'too old,' if she is emotionally upset by pregnancy, or if pregnancy interferes with schooling or career, the law considers those situations as 'health' reasons for abortion. In other words, as you know and we know, an exception for 'health' means abortion on demand."

The archbishops of Chicago, Philadelphia, Washington, Baltimore, Boston, Los Angeles, Detroit, and New York, along with the president of the National Conference of Catholic Bishops, signed the letter. They saw President Clinton's veto as taking "our nation to a critical turning point in its treatment of helpless human beings inside and outside the womb. It moves our nation one step further toward acceptance of infanticide. Combined with the two recent federal appeals court decisions seeking to legitimize assisted suicide, it sounds the alarm that public officials are moving our society ever more rapidly to embrace a culture of death."

Partial Birth Abortion Ban legislation, very close to its original form, was reintroduced in the next session of Congress. The lobbying, hearings, and outcome were the same. By October 8, 1997, the bill had passed both houses of Congress. The health exception was not included. President Clinton issued his veto on October 10, 1997. Again, among supporters of the ban, there was an outcry of dismay, sorrow, and disgust. Those seeking to strengthen respect for the health, autonomy and integrity of mothers, fathers, their families and physicians breathed yet another sigh of relief. While passage of the bill had garnered more support, it was still a few votes shy of what was needed to override the president's veto (i.e., House of Representatives: 295–136; Senate: 64–36).

The Political Landscape

By this time, the issue of abortion had long been a central pillar of political campaigns. President Clinton and Congress were seemingly not far apart. Disagreement remained on exemptions for health consequences. National public opinion polls painted a mixed picture, but when specifications were included in the questions about the mother's health and physician's involvement the nation was fairly evenly split (Saad 2002). Some 30 states passed legislation in one way or another banning partial-birth abortions. Wording used in these statutes reflected a coordinated, national agenda. The outlawed procedures focused on D&X procedures Dr. Haskell had outlined. For the most part, these statutory bans did not include other late-term procedures such as D&E, infusion or induction methods. The politics of using the "partial-birth" wording yielded legislation focused on procedure and location of the unborn, not on outcome.

A Strange and Strained Argument

Dismembering the unborn fetus *in utero*, as was done using D&E procedures, or employing the various "softening" techniques of other procedures, were by in large not covered by the state statutes or the proposed federal legislation. Instead, while specific wording differed here and there, the focus was vaginal placement of a substantial portion of the unborn child for the purpose of performing procedures the physician knew would kill the child.

The state statutes were challenged in court. The first to reach the Supreme Court came from Nebraska in *Stenberg v. Carhart* (2000). It had been challenged just two days after its passage. On June 28, 2000, in the midst of a closely contested presidential campaign, the Supreme Court handed down an aggressively argued 5–4 decision declaring the Nebraska law unconstitutional. Two reasons were given. Most obviously, the Nebraska statute lacked an exception for protecting the "health" of the mother. Five of the Court's nine justices found that this omission violated precedents set out in *Roe, Doe,* and *Casey.* In addition, the definition and description of what Nebraska legislators had in mind by "partial-birth abortion" procedures was deemed too ambiguous.

There had always been potential confusion between D&X and D&E procedures. Dr. Haskell had noted the link when describing how the fortuitous location of a foot, meant the fetus could be easily pulled into the birth canal. The Nebraska statute focused on D&X procedures, but included "deliberately and intentionally delivering into the vagina a living unborn child, *or a substantial portion thereof* (emphasis added), for the purpose of performing a procedure that the person performing such procedure knows will kill the unborn child and does kill the unborn child."

What did "substantial portion" mean? A foot? Two legs? The torso? In his oral argument before the Court, Nebraska's Attorney General pointed to legislative debate for clarification. One senator had asked the bill's sponsor, "[Y]ou said that as small a portion of the fetus as a foot would constitute a substantial portion in your opinion. Is that correct?" The sponsoring senator had agreed, "Yes, I believe that's correct." This being the case, D&E and D&X procedures shaded into one another. Surely, protected life should not depend solely on the chance location of a foot. What happened if a D&E procedure turned into D&X while the abortion was taking place? The majority of the Court concluded there was too much overlap. This left physicians at risk of prosecution and the woman with too few acceptable options, creating a "substantial obstacle" and an "undue burden" on her choices in violation of the Court's findings in *Casey.*

When it came to defining the protective boundaries of life, this was a strange and strained argument. Nebraska's law was unacceptable because it did not specify clearly where the fetus was when life was taken. Justice Scalia, writing in dissent, and referring to D&X procedures as "live-birth" abortions, berated the majority's rationale, noting that overturning Nebraska's ban on "this visibly brutal means of eliminating our half-born posterity is quite simply absurd." Justice O'Connor, disagreeing and concurring with the majority, noted that if the statute had been limited to D&X procedures and included a health exception, "the question presented would be quite different." Given the question posed, however, their reasoning was sound.

Sound or absurd, the vote was 5–4 and the ruling was released. Nebraska's statute banning partial-birth abortions was overturned. Given similar wording in statutes in more than two-dozen other states (estimates varied, depending on how the wording was interpreted), the impact was national. Those working to ban partial birth abortions were dealt a serious setback. The battle to determine when early life was fully protected, however, was not over.

Proponents for the ban took lessons from the Supreme Court's assessment of Nebraska's law. These lessons would influence their next steps. In November 2000, George W. Bush was elected president, by the narrowest of margins. On December 12, 2000, the Supreme Court certified his election some six months after Nebraska's *Stenberg* decision. While his administration would be consumed with other matters, President Bush was far more sympathetic, indeed, committed to, the banning of partial-birth abortions than was his predecessor.

The Political Landscape Shifts

By October 2003, taking into account the Court's assessment of the Nebraska statute, federal legislation was revised, hearings held, amendments considered, revisions made and votes taken. The Partial-Birth Abortion Ban Act of 2003 did not contain a health exception for the mother, but it did clarify various other issues. It passed both houses of Congress by wide margins.[1] President Bush, on November 5, 2003, signed the Act into law.

At the signing ceremony the president underscored his strong support, grounded in reverence for all young lives. "The best case against partial birth abortion," he said, "is a simple description of what happens and to whom it happens. It involves the partial delivery of a live boy or girl, and a sudden, violent end of that life. Our nation owes its children a different and better welcome. (Applause.) The bill I am about to sign protecting innocent new life from this practice reflects the compassion and humanity of America."

---

1   In the Senate the initial vote was 64–33–3. The House of Representatives passed its version without objection, but there were differences with the Senate. These were worked out, and on October 2, 2003, a vote of 281–142–12 was recorded. The Senate then voted in support 64–34–2.

During the signing ceremony, President Bush may or may not have been aware of experiences such as those Gretchen Voss (2004) wrote about a few months later in the *Boston Globe*. She and her husband, Dave, had gone to see ultrasound images of their developing baby. "As images of our baby filled the black screen, we oohed and aahed like the goofy expectant parents." From the technician's expression, however, it soon became evident something was wrong. A few minutes later the expectant parents were meeting with their doctor. The ultrasound image had revealed the fetus had an open neural tube defect. The extent of the problem was not clear and they were advised to go to another hospital in Boston for further diagnosis.

The news was not good. "Instead of cinnamon and spice, our child came with technical terms like hydrocephalus and spina bifida. The spine, she [the doctor] said, had not closed properly, and because of the location of the opening, it was as bad as it got. What they knew—that the baby would certainly be paralyzed and incontinent, that the baby's brain was being tugged against the opening in the base of the skull and the cranium was full of fluid—was awful. What they didn't know—whether the baby would live at all, and if so, with what sort of mental and developmental defects—was devastating. Countless surgeries would be required if the baby did live. None of them would repair the damage that was already done."

For Gretchen and Dave, the Partial Birth Abortion Ban Act of 2003 did not reflect life affirming compassion but a callous, misguided attempt to prohibit humane responses to deeply personal tragedies. "President Bush's attempt to ban partial-birth abortions threatens all late-term procedures. But in my case, everyone said it was the right thing to do—even my Catholic father and Republican father-in-law.... Though the baby might live, it was not a life that we would choose for our child, a child that we already loved. We decided to terminate the pregnancy. It was our last parental decision." Later, after Dave's brother had left a tearful message on their answering machine, Gretchen found her husband, "kneeling on the floor in our bathroom, doubled over and bawling, his body quaking."

Life and suffering, boundaries and dilemmas—there were no truly satisfying answers. Still proponents on both sides pressed forward. The question now became whether the new federal statute, lacking as it did an exception for the mother's health, would clear the constitutional hurdle any better than the Nebraska law.

Legal Details

Drafters had gone to great lengths to ensure it would. The omission of a "health" exception, however, seemed to fly in the face of the Nebraska ruling. The omission was intentional. The congressional reasoning was blunt. The first paragraph of the Act read, "A moral, medical, and ethical consensus exists that the practice of performing a partial-birth abortion ... is a gruesome and inhumane procedure that is never medically necessary and should be prohibited." Congress based this blanket claim on hearings it had held.

From these hearings it was concluded, "Congress finds that partial-birth abortion is never medically indicated to preserve the health of the mother; is in fact unrecognized as a valid abortion procedure by the mainstream medical community; poses additional health risks to the mother; blurs the line between abortion and infanticide in the killing of a partially-born child just inches from birth; and confuses the role of the physician in childbirth and should, therefore, be banned." Congress had made a major effort to develop the factual basis for this conclusion through sworn testimony. Their well-developed findings deserved the Court's deference. There was no need for a "health" exception. Others would disagree—the findings were not at all clear-cut and should be questioned.

The second problem the Supreme Court had found with the Nebraska statute was the meaning of the phrase "substantial portion" of the fetus outside the womb. How much was enough? Also of concern was the chance that what started as a common D&E procedure might unintentionally become a partial-birth, D&X. To deal with these issues, Congress included quite specific wording.

> The term 'partial-birth abortion' means an abortion in which ... the person performing the abortion deliberately and intentionally vaginally delivers a living fetus until, in the case of a head-first presentation, the entire fetal head is outside the body of the mother, or, in the case of breech presentation, any part of the fetal trunk past the navel is outside the body of the mother for the purpose of performing an overt act that the person knows will kill the partially delivered living fetus.

Clearly, there were now specific anatomical landmarks for the protected boundaries of life. In the case of head-first presentation, the full head must be outside the mother's body. In the case of a breech presentation, it was beyond the navel.

The rationale for these markers was not provided, nor were the reasons for why this type of abortion was more "gruesome" and "inhumane" than the D&E *in utero* dismemberment. The lines, however, had been drawn. Those who voted for the Act and the president who signed it into law believed they had found the "bright line" between abortion and infanticide, and had struck the appropriate balance among the competing values involving the woman's health.

It remained for the courts to decide. The response was immediate. The day President Bush signed the Act, cases were brought almost simultaneously to the U.S. district courts in Northern California, Southern New York, and Nebraska. Citing well-known precedent, all three district courts found the Partial Birth Abortion Ban Act of 2003 unconstitutional. There was continuing concern about whether the Act imposed undue constraints on the woman's choices, but most important was concern for the omission of any consideration given to exceptions for the woman's health. This was unacceptable.

When Attorney General, Alberto Gonzales, appealed these rulings to the relevant circuit courts, the outcome was the same. All three found the Act unconstitutional. In the Nebraska case, the circuit court noted, Congressional claims notwithstanding, "If one thing is clear from the record in this case, it is that no consensus exists in the medical community." In this situation, "… the Constitution requires legislatures to err on the side of protecting women's health by including a health exception." The conclusion followed, as night follows day. "Because the Act does not contain a health exception, it is unconstitutional."

By the end of January 2006, a total of six district and circuit court opinions, relying on the Supreme Court's findings in *Stenberg* and other supporting cases, now agreed in outcome. The Act signed into law by President Bush was unconstitutional. The Attorney General appealed to the Supreme Court. The Court agreed to hear the Nebraska case in February 2006 and combined it with the case from California in June. While the parallels between the new federal law and the earlier Nebraska statute already declared unconstitutional by the Supreme Court were clear, there were important differences. The original *Stenberg decision* had been razor-thin—5 to 4. It had been aggressively argued, with strong dissents. The new federal Act had addressed at least some of the concerns. Attorney General Gonzales was hopeful the outcome would be different.

It had been seven years since the Nebraska case had been decided. Two justices, who had participated in that case, were no longer on the court. Justice Alito had replaced Justice O'Connor, who had voted to strike down the Nebraska law. John Roberts, the attorney who had argued before the Supreme Court on behalf of the Summer of Mercy protestors, had replaced Chief Justice Rehnquist, who had found the earlier Nebraska law constitutional. With these two new justices siding with the majority, the Supreme Court, again voting 5–4, found the constitutional shortcomings of the earlier Nebraska statue had been overcome. The Partial Birth Abortion Ban Act of 2003 met constitutional standards.[2]

Justice Kennedy, who had written a dissenting opinion when the Nebraska law was overturned, wrote for the majority. The concerns regarding overlap in D&X and D&E procedures, so evident in the Nebraska law, had been remedied. Intentional action was required. The protected boundaries of life had been specified. Depending on a head-

---

2   The votes in the two cases were: *Stenberg v. Carhart*: For the Majority: Breyer joined by Stevens, O'Connor, Souter, Ginsburg; Dissent: Kennedy joined by Rehnquist, Scalia, Thomas. *Gonzales v. Carhart*: For the Majority: Kennedy joined by Roberts, Scalia, Thomas, Alito; Dissent: Ginsburg, joined Stevens, Souter, Breyer.

first or breech delivery, the anatomical markers were clear. They were the baby's head or navel.

What about balancing the need to protect the mother's health? This was totally missing in the Partial Birth Abortion Ban Act of 2003. Courts at all levels, including the Supreme Court, had previously underscored its importance numerous times. This go-around, contradictory medical testimony regarding the issue had been heard throughout the appeals process as well as in final oral arguments before the Supreme Court. Unlike the circuit courts, where it was held that in such uncertain circumstances legislatures should "err on the side of protecting women's health," Justice Kennedy and colleagues voting with him were more willing to tolerate uncertainty. They wrote, "The Act is not invalid on its face where there is uncertainty over whether the barred procedure is ever necessary to preserve a woman's health." In such circumstances, remedies should be sought in an "as-applied challenge." Threats to the mother's health would have to be decided on a case-by-case basis. She and her doctor would have to ask for an exception to the law before proceeding with D&X procedures.

This was new. Writing in dissent, Justice Ruth Bader Ginsburg found this "piecemeal" approach "gravely mistaken" in that it jeopardized the woman's health and put the physician in an "untenable position." She also found portions of the all-male majority's vote to be a chauvinistic throwback to an earlier time. The Court had heard in oral argument that doctors were sometimes reluctant to provide their patients with full information about the D&X procedures, desiring to shield them from the graphic details.

In a textbook example of **paternalism**, they wanted to protect her, even if her own values and assessment of the situation differed from theirs. Ironically, they grounded their concern in the mother's mental health. Justice Kennedy wrote, "It is self-evident that a mother who comes to regret her choice to abort must struggle with grief more anguished and sorrow more profound when she learns, only after the event, what she once did not know: that she allowed a doctor to pierce the skull and vacuum the fast-developing brain of her unborn child, a child assuming the human form." These procedures should be banned to protect the mother from her own faulty, ill-informed judgment.

The single remaining woman on the Court, joined by three of her male colleagues, found this reasoning inappropriate and condescending. It reflected, Justice Ginsburg noted, "ancient notions about women's place in the family and under the Constitution—ideas that have long since been discredited." Citing *Casey*, she reminded her brethren that they had previously found the "destiny of the woman must be shaped … on her own conception of her spiritual imperatives and her place in society." Further, Justice Ginsburg noted, the means "chosen by the State to further the interest in potential life must be calculated to inform the woman's free choice, not hinder it." The tension remained. This time, however, the razor-thin 5–4 majority fell on the side of banning, not the taking of life late in pregnancy, but on the location of the fetus and a specified abortion procedure.

Adapting to a Strange and Strained Decision

The Partial Birth Abortion Ban Act of 2003 was now the law of the land. Like the earlier decision in *Stenberg*, this was a strange and strained decision. It did not protect life. It simply affirmed the banning of a procedure based on the location of the fetus. It did not demand exceptions for the mother's health, though paternalistically it did express concern for her mental anguish should she change her mind. The now established legal boundary for protected life was whether the unborn child had been intentionally drawn out of the womb past its head or beyond its navel when its life was ended.

Mothers, their physicians, and supporting hospital abortion policies adapted. A few months later the *Boston Globe* reported (Goldberg 2007), "In response to the Supreme Court decision upholding the Partial-Birth Abortion Ban Act, many abortion providers in Boston and around the country have adopted a defensive tactic. To avoid any chance of partially delivering a live fetus, they are injecting fetuses with lethal drugs before procedures." In some hospitals, the article continued, these alternatives had become policy. "Three major Harvard-affiliated hospitals—Massachusetts General, Brigham and Women's, and Beth Israel Deaconess—have responded to the ban by making the injections the new standard operating procedure for abortions beginning at around 20 weeks' gestation ... Boston Medical Center, too, has begun using injections for later surgical abortions ... The decision came 'after a lot of anguish about what to do.'"

While the Partial Birth Abortion Ban Act of 2003 established anatomical markers for the protected boundaries of life, it did not provide a quality-of-life rationale for why these markers were chosen. More recently, a number of states (including Nebraska, Idaho, Indiana, Kansas, Oklahoma, and Alabama) have turned not to the viability of the fetus or its location in the birth canal, but to the capacity of the fetus to feel pain. Once this capacity was present, the unborn child, it is argued, crosses into the realm of protected life. Advocates for this boundary for protected life set the time around the 20th week of gestation. "The purpose of this type of bill is to focus on the humanity of the unborn child ... Fetal pain is something that people who are in the middle on the abortion issue can relate to" (Mary Spaulding Balch quoted in Eckholm 2001). There is debate, however, over when a fetus is actually able to experience pain, and exceptions to the 20-week limit are made when carrying a pregnancy to term might result in death or serious physical impairment for the mother. No exceptions are made for other medical or mental health threats to the mother, for the late discovery of serious disabilities of the fetus, or for pregnancies that are the result of rape or incest.

If a threshold based on the capacity to feel pain is established and a child is protected once it emerges up to her navel or past his head, the protected status of an infant's life, fully born, would appear to be settled. Questions, however, remain. Following birth, these questions swirl around the child's mental and physical capacities and projections of whether the just-born child will have a life worth living, protecting, and supporting.

DISCUSSION QUESTIONS

1. Under what conditions, if any, should late-term abortions be legal? Describe the reasons for the position you take.
2. What is a "partial-birth abortion"? What effect might describing a late-term abortion in this way have on support or opposition for abortion?
3. Describe the challenges associated with determining when an abortion is a "partial-birth abortion."
4. A number of serious problems cannot be detected until quite late in a pregnancy. Should parents in these circumstances be allowed to decide to terminate their pregnancy?
5. How have the practices of abortion providers changed as a result of limitations on late-term abortions?

V: Should the Baby Live?

It was a long-established principle of law that infants born alive were considered persons, fully entitled to the protections of the law. But, as the twentieth century drew to a close, Representative Charles T. Canady, Chairman of the House Judiciary Subcommittee on the Constitution, was concerned. He saw "changes in the legal and cultural landscape" and what was increasingly referred to as an emerging "culture of death" (see, for example, Smith 2000). He aimed to clarify through proposed legislation, the Born-Alive Protection Act of 2000.

Introducing his legislation, Canady explained his concerns. "The principle that born-alive infants are entitled to the protection of the law is being questioned at one of America's most prestigious universities." Princeton University bioethicist Peter Singer, Canady noted was arguing "that parents should have the option to kill disabled or unhealthy newborn babies for a certain period after birth." This was based on Professor Singer's view that "the life of a newborn baby is 'of no greater value than the life of a nonhuman animal at a similar level of rationality, self-consciousness, awareness, capacity to feel, etc.'" According to Professor Singer, Representative Canady noted, "'killing a disabled infant is not morally equivalent to killing a person. Very often it is not wrong at all.'"

Representative Canady went on to recount the implications of Singer's argument in the recent tragic treatment of an infant on the "outskirts of viability." The purpose of his bill, he told his congressional colleagues, was "to repudiate the pernicious ideas that result in tragedies such as this and to firmly establish that, for purposes of federal law, an infant who is completely expelled or extracted from her mother and who is alive is, indeed, a person under the law."

Representative Canady concluded his prepared statement with a specific proposal. As clear and specific as Canady's proposed legislation seemed to be, some minor opposition remained. Final amendments were worked out, and President George W. Bush signed the all but unanimously passed Born Alive Infants Protection Act into law on August 5, 2002. By the time the Act was signed into law, almost three decades had passed since the *Roe* and *Doe* decisions. An estimated 40 states had already passed related "born alive" legislation. Over this period, the questions motivating this broad-based legal reform movement had been posed, answered, and re-answered numerous times over. Why so much effort to resolve such a seemingly obvious question?

Lives Worth Living, Protecting, and Supporting

Concern was raised shortly after *Roe,* when James Watson, agreeing with his colleague Francis Crick, conjectured, "If a child were not declared alive until three days after birth … The doctor could allow the child to die if the parents so chose and save a lot of misery and suffering. I believe this view is the only rational, compassionate attitude to have" (Watson 1973). A professor at American University, Jeffrey Reiman joined the fray and articulated his rationale: "Killing children or adults is wrong," Reiman wrote, "because of properties *they* possess; killing infants [is wrong], because of an emotion that *we* naturally and rightly have toward infants" (Reiman 1999: 108). For many the implications of his distinction were illusive.

Reiman elaborated (1999: 108). It was a matter of empathy. We might love, identify with, and desire to protect infants, but infants "do not possess in their own right a property that makes it wrong to kill them." It followed that while empathy and emotional attachments should be honored, "there will be permissible exceptions to the rule against killing [infants] that will not apply to the rule against killing adults or children." In particular, Reiman continued, "I think (as do many philosophers, doctors, and parents) that ending the lives of severely handicapped newborns will be acceptable." He left blurred the exact boundary separating less protected infancy from fully protected children and adults. He was also unclear on the precise meaning of "handicapped newborns." Fully protected life depended on when and whether the infant possessed self-awareness and other attributes of "personhood" or "humanhood."[1]

No one, however, had more thoroughly, provocatively, and carefully explored the protective boundaries of early life and how some lives might be more worthy than others of living, protecting, and supporting than Peter Singer. Writing in 1985, Singer and his colleague Helga Kuhse introduced their book, *Should the Baby Live? The Problem of Handicapped Infants,* with the bluntly provocative statement, "This book contains conclusions which some readers will find disturbing. We think that some infants with severe disabilities should be killed."

It was an intentionally jarring, directly stated claim. It had drawn a good deal of attention. It was grounded in the belief that the level of suffering must be taken into account and weighed in the balance against the duty to prolong and protect life. In some circumstances, the most humane course of action was to terminate an infant's life with care and compassion. Some lives, some moments and manifestations of life, were seen as more worthy of protection and support than others. We might want to deny this, we might think it morally wrong, there might be deeply troubling

---

1 See Fletcher 1954; Tooley 1972: 37–65; Ramsey 1978; Engelhardt, Jr. 1996, especially Chapter 4.

ethical implications reminiscent of Nazi atrocities, but there was ample evidence for the ubiquitous presence of such actions based on these beliefs.

For Kuhse and Singer (1985), such actions could be justified and should be defended. They built their argument by first reviewing the cases of two babies. Both had Down Syndrome. In both instances the parents decided to let their child die. The first case occurred in 1980, in Derby, England, the second in Bloomington, Indiana, in 1982.

In Derby, shortly after the birth of her child, the mother was overheard by one of her sisters saying tearfully to her husband, "I don't want it, Duck." The doctor was informed and acceded to the parents' wishes. He wrote in the baby's records "Parents do not wish baby to survive. Nursing care only." He also prescribed a pain-killing drug to ease the child's suffering. It turned out this drug may have hastened death. Two days later, the infant was reported to be restless and struggling for breath. Early in the morning of the third day he died in the arms of a nurse.

A troubled member of the hospital staff reported the doctor's actions to an advocacy organization. Members of the organization went to the police. The doctor was charged with murder. This charge was later reduced to attempted murder as the baby had developed pneumonia, and it was unclear whether the baby had died from this or the doctor's action.

After a brief trial, the judge outlined several examples he felt might help the jury work through the legal and ethical issues defining the line between properly letting a patient die and unlawful murder. In reaching their decision, the jury's rationale remains unknown. They may have believed the doctor was not attempting to kill the child, but rather to alleviate suffering. They may have simply substituted their own moral judgment and negated the law in an exercise of jury nullification. Whatever the rationale, two hours after deliberations began, jurors returned with their verdict: Not guilty.

In the Bloomington case, there was a complicating physical condition, frequently associated with Down Syndrome. For the baby to survive, a relatively simple operation with a high probability of success was necessary to remove a blockage in the infant's digestive tract. It would not affect the underlying mental handicap, but the child could be expected to lead an otherwise normal life.

The mother and father were in their early thirties. They had experience working with children with this condition. Both parents were of the opinion that such children "never had a minimally acceptable quality of life." They also had other children at home, whom they wanted and needed to support. After consulting with their physicians, they decided not to give permission for the operation.

The hospital doctors and administrators contacted a local judge, asking for a ruling. The judge sided with the parents. The baby was now three days old and a decision was made not to appeal the judge's ruling. The local prosecutor, however, asked the judge to order intravenous feeding to keep the baby alive, at least temporarily. The judge refused. The prosecutor took his pleas for intervention to the State Supreme Court. Again, in support of parental autonomy, the answer was "No." Learning of the case, a number of families called the hospital and filed petitions with the court offering to adopt the baby. These requests were denied. The prosecutor, accompanied by a law professor from Indiana University, flew to Washington, D.C. seeking emergency intervention from the U.S. Supreme Court. While in route to plead their case, the infant, now six days old, died.

Word spread immediately about the Bloomington case, producing an outcry among those who could not understand how the parents might let their child die and how physicians and the courts would stand idly by. One widely read newspaper columnist was a father of a child with Down Syndrome. Writing a week after "Baby Doe" in Bloomington had died, George Will stated unequivocally how "common sense and common usage require use of the word 'homicide'." In addition to his consternation and condemnation of what had happened, Will wanted his readers to know of and learn from the childhood joys experienced by his son:

> Jonathan Will, 10, fourth-grader and Orioles fan (and the best Wiffle-ball hitter in southern Maryland), has Down's syndrome. He does not "suffer from" (as newspapers are wont to say) Down's syndrome. He suffers from nothing, except anxiety about the Orioles' lousy start.
>
> He is doing nicely, thank you. But he is bound to have quite enough problems dealing with society—receiving rights, let alone empathy. He can do without people like Infant Doe's parents, and courts like Indiana's asserting by their actions the principle that people like him are less than fully human. On the evidence, Down's syndrome citizens have little to learn about being human from the people responsible for the death of Infant Doe.
>
> (Will 1982: A29)

As compelling as his son's story was, not all parents agreed. Their children with Down Syndrome had not been so fortunate. One couple, living in Santa Barbara, California, replied. Unlike Will, they identified with the Bloomington parents. They too, "after much agonizing thought, prayer and discussion with family, friends, clergymen and other doctors," had made "the same painful decision ..." In their case, however, the hospital authorities did not cooperate. They knew how to successfully replace their son's missing esophagus and were going to proceed with or without the parents' consent. A court order was obtained and the surgery performed. The outcome was not good.

> Our baby has endured a great deal of pain, suffering and misery during his 18 months on Earth, due to the nature of his deformities, surgical procedures, and complications arising from them.

He is not well today and is unable to eat orally. The doctors have told us there is a good probability that our son will suffer from lifelong problems … It is indeed difficult to stand by and watch this occur.

(cited in Kuhse and Singer 1985: 16)

Regulations Emerge

George Will had helped craft the successful campaign of President Ronald Reagan. He remained close to the Reagan White House. A week after Will's column appeared, President Reagan issued memoranda to relevant federal agencies requesting that policies to prevent recurrences such as those in Bloomington be devised.[2]

President Reagan's orders were grounded in a law passed in 1973 that forbade agencies receiving federal funds from withholding services ordinarily provided handicapped citizens. In his communication with the Attorney General, President Reagan noted, "Our nation's commitment to equal protection of the law will have little meaning if we deny such protection to those who have not been blessed with the same physical or mental gifts we too often take for granted."

It is important to recall how rapidly the rhetoric surrounding these matters was shifting. It was common through the 1950s to use the terms moron, imbecile, and idiot, or even monstrosities at birth, to characterize children not blessed with the same physical or mental gifts we too often take for granted. In his influential but much criticized, *Morals and Medicine*, published in 1954, Episcopal clergyman Joseph Fletcher had reviewed the arguments of "those who favor involuntary euthanasia for monstrosities at birth," noting in a footnote, "It has always been a quite common practice of midwives and, in modern times, doctors, simply to fail to respirate monstrous babies at birth" (Fletcher 1954: 207).

Two years later, in 1956, a noted Cambridge University jurist, Glanville Williams, used similar terms. He had given a series of lectures at Columbia University. These were published in somewhat revised form in *The Sanctity of Life and the Criminal Law*. In a chapter titled "The Protection of Human Life" Glanville noted, again in the dehumanizing parlance of the day, "There is, indeed, some kind of legal argument that a 'monster' is not protected under the existing law." Williams then went on to note, "Fortunately, the question whether a monster is human has small practical importance for the most extreme cases, because the acephalous, ectocardiac, etc., monster will usually die quickly after birth" (Williams 1957: 20–24).

---

2 The genesis of President Reagan's several orders are somewhat unclear. See Brown 1986: 234.

By the 1980s, medical technology and greater sensitivity to civil discourse were changing both the probability of death and the rhetoric used. Medical technology had greatly enhanced the life chances of many of these infants and deepened our understanding of the underlying genesis of birth defects. While the dehumanizing "monster" reference disappeared from legal and moral discourse, disagreements over the boundaries of protected life for otherwise imperiled infants remained.

The initial regulations following President Reagan's orders were hurriedly constructed. They were revised almost immediately to provide an oxymoronic "Interim Final Rule," which took effect March 22, 1983. They referred vaguely to "handicapped infants." They called for posters to be displayed in "a conspicuous place in each delivery ward." These posters were to carry the message that failure to feed and care for handicapped infants was a violation of federal law and that "Any person having knowledge that a handicapped infant is being discriminatorily denied food or customary medical care" should contact a Handicapped Infant Hotline. A phone number in Washington D.C. was provided.

A good deal of confusion and suspicion followed. Critics began referring to the absurdity of Baby Doe Squads being dispatched from the nation's capital to hospital delivery wards all across the nation in response to anonymous phone calls. Within two weeks suits were filed and injunctions sought by numerous professional associations, including the American Hospital Association and the American Academy of Pediatrics. The major complaints were focused: The federal government had no standing to intervene. The guidelines for treatment were too vague and had been drafted through inappropriate procedures.

A pediatrician practicing in New Mexico reported, "Because of the fear I had in being 'reported,' I recently spent one agonizing hour trying to resuscitate a newborn who had no larynx, and many other congenital anomalies. The sad part was that both the parents in the delivery room watched this most difficult ordeal. It was obvious to me that this was in no way a viable child but I felt compelled to carry on this way out of fear someone in the hospital would 'turn me in.' I am sure that you who sit in Washington are not faced with such difficult decisions at two o'clock a.m." (cited in Kuhse and Singer 1985: 43).

The more general point was the lack of recognition that not all handicaps were as minor as those faced by Jonathan Will or Baby Doe in Bloomington, Indiana. What about a "handicap" where the child was born with most of her brain missing? What about a condition known as intra-cranial hemorrhage, where the child might never breathe without a respirator and never have the capacity for cognition? What about a condition where a substantial portion of the digestive tract was missing, leaving an infant without the ability to digest food?

For many, including Jeffrey Reiman, Helga Kuhse, and Peter Singer, such handicaps raised questions about whether a life truly worth living, prolonging, and protecting was present. Medical treatment might be futile and serve no other end than prolonging the baby's suffering. Sometimes we might simply want to let an infant die, even hasten its death, as peacefully and as comfortably as possible. The intention to let life go is profoundly different from the intention to destroy it. The boundaries of tolerable suffering, like the boundaries of protected life, would have to be more carefully drawn. Dilemmas infused with forced tragic choices between protecting life and alleviating suffering could not be avoided.

Nagging Uncertainties—Who Should Decide?

The courts agreed with those bringing the suit against the proposed **Baby Doe Guidelines**. As the regulations were being revised yet again, this time allowing specified exceptions,[3] a young baby girl, soon to be known as "Baby Jane Doe," was born on October 11, 1983, in Port Jefferson, Long Island, New York. She was the first child of a young couple, married about a year, born with numerous interrelated physical and mental defects including spina bifida, kidney damage, microcephaly, a condition associated with incomplete brain development, and hydrocephaly, where fluid accumulates in the brain, sometimes causing brain damage.

Her physicians recommended operations to deal with the manifestations of spina bifida and to reduce the fluid in her skull. If performed, these operations might lengthen her life from a matter of weeks or months to perhaps 20 years or more. However long the life, there were risks and uncertainties all along the way. The child, in all likelihood, would be severely retarded, epileptic, paralyzed, and subject to infections. Baby Jane Doe's parents decided, after consulting with their clergy and attending physicians, to forego the operations and simply ensure that their baby girl was made comfortable and free from infection. Given the many uncertainties they faced, their physicians agreed.

The course of treatment would have been set had it not been for a lawyer in Vermont, Lawrence Washburn, Jr., a dedicated pro-life activist and total stranger to the family. Given his convictions and commitments, he filed suit with a New York Judge who had been the Right-to-Life party's candidate when he ran for the judgeship the previous year (Annas 1984). The judge appointed a guardian who stated at the subsequent hearing he thought the physicians and parents were wrong, arguing instead for immediate treatment. The judge agreed and so ordered.

The parents took the case to New York's Court of Appeals. With the appellate judges labeling Washburn's law suit "distressing and offensive," the court found that the

---

3 These exceptions were: (1) The infant is chronically and irreversibly comatose; (2) The provision of such treatment would merely prolong dying, not be effective in ameliorating or correcting all of the infant's life-threatening conditions, or otherwise be futile in terms of the survival of the infant; or (3) The provision of such treatment would be virtually futile in terms of the survival of the infant and the treatment itself under such circumstances would be inhumane.

parents had made "these decisions with love and thoughtfulness, and that strangers, however whimsical or well-intentioned, cannot subject them to this outrageous kind of proceeding."

As the case wound its way through the courts, publicity followed and the parents agreed to an interview on *60 Minutes* (March 11: 1984) with Ed Bradley. Bradley asked the infant's mother, "How do you feel when someone else who didn't know you, didn't know the child, had no connection with your family went to court to make a decision about your child's life?" With obvious emotion, she responded, "I think it is unbelievable. They don't have any right at all. They don't know our child. They don't love her. We are her parents. We are the only ones who can make this decision for her."

The father was of like mind: "It was very frightening to hear that a total stranger could force us into a state supreme court to answer for our decision making ... It is very hard to understand his concern about our daughter's life when after all the court proceedings have ended, he would no longer be around, or heard from, or there to care for our daughter."

Washburn, who still had not met the parents or their struggling child, was unmoved. He responded in a subsequent interview that he remained convinced in the rightness of his actions, believing profoundly retarded children were the children of a good God, given to us because as call to heroism, and greatness (Chambers 1983). The case was taken to the U.S. Supreme Court where judges declined, without comment, to review. New York's Court of Appeals decision and the parents' autonomy stood. Other accompanying issues, however, remained unresolved.

While Washburn was preparing his suit and proceedings were progressing, an anonymous caller had used the U.S. Department of Health and Human Services' (HHS) "hotline" to complain about the discriminatory treatment being given to Baby Jane Doe. In response, the case was referred to child protective services, where it was concluded there was no cause for intervention. Surgeon General, C. Everett Koop, a pediatric surgeon closely aligned with the pro-life political movement, however, disagreed and wanted to examine the medical records.

Three weeks following Baby Jane Doe's birth, on November 6, Surgeon General Koop appeared on the national television show, *Face the Nation,* to discuss his involvement in the case and his decision to request related medical records. He had made similar requests for access in some 48 other cases. The focus was not on Baby Jane Doe but on the greater good. "We're not just fighting for this baby," he said. "We're fighting for the principle of this country that every life is individually and uniquely sacred." "[T]wo different surgeons said different things." Koop noted. "One said, 'Operate. Operate now.' One said, 'Don't operate at all.' I think when you have that kind of a difference of opinion, there ought to be an independent review, there ought to be a third opinion" (see Bird 1983; Van Den Haag and Washington 1984).

The parents, doctors, and hospital felt they had reviewed the case appropriately and quite enough, and refused to provide the baby's medical records. A suit on behalf of HHS was filed to obtain them.

U.S. Supreme Court agreed to review the case in *Bowen v American Hosp. Ass'n* (1986). The basic rationale for the Baby Doe Guidelines once again came under review. Some three years after Baby Jane Doe was born, in *Bowen* the Court found, "The Secretary's [of HHS] own summaries of these cases establish beyond doubt that the respective hospitals did not withhold medical care on the basis of handicap ... as a result, they provide no support for his claim that federal regulation is needed in order to forestall comparable cases in the future."

The opinion continued, "Concerned and loving parents had chosen one appropriate medical course over another." They had made an informed decision that was "in the best interests of the infant." The U.S. Supreme Court, as the New York Court of Appeals had done before them, affirmed parental autonomy to decide what was in the best interest of their handicapped child. Absent evidence of abuse, the government should stay out of these matters and decisions should remain close to home.

When Doctors Say No

The cases that so bothered George Will, President Ronald Reagan, Lawrence Washburn, and C. Everett Koop had led to the **Baby Doe Regulations**. These regulations were initially grounded in civil rights era legislation prohibiting discrimination against the handicapped. Subsequent revisions shifted justification of governmental oversight to evidence of child abuse and neglect. Whatever the justification, these regulations had evolved from cases where parents refused consent for treatment of their newly born infants. What if parents wanted treatment for their child and their physicians refused?

This question was raised in *Bowen*. It was dismissed as too remote a possibility for serious consideration. Justices writing in the majority chided their dissenting colleagues for "speculating about nonexistent hypothetical cases in which a hospital might refuse to provide treatment requested by parents." If there was need for the Baby Doe Regulations, surveys of doctors showed and the Court concluded, it was "because parents refuse consent to treatment and physicians acquiesce." The idea that doctors might refuse to treat infants with parental pleas to do so seemed far-fetched.

As medical technology continued to advance and medical care became increasingly expensive, however, the remote possibility became increasingly real. On October 13, 1992, in Falls Church, Virginia, a baby girl was born lacking a major portion of her brain. While she was still in her mother's womb, **anencephaly** had been detected. The early indicators were severe enough that both the obstetrician and neonatologist, counseled the mother to terminate her pregnancy (Annas 1994). They sensed the follow-on care would be quite expensive, the baby's life would be profoundly limited, and perhaps not worth living.

The mother disagreed and her daughter was born. As predicted, the infant lacked a major portion of her brain, skull, and scalp. Her brain stem supported her autonomic functions and reflex actions, but without a cerebrum she was permanently unconscious. She was unable to see or hear, she lacked all cognitive abilities, and was unaware of and otherwise unable to interact with her environment. There was no known medical treatment that would improve her "vegetative" condition.

Anencephalic infants generally die within a few days after birth due to breathing difficulties or other complications. When the baby's breathing became labored, mechanical ventilation was started, in part to allow the doctors time to explain more fully the baby's prospects to her mother (the father was only marginally involved.) Within a few days, the physicians were urging that the artificial ventilation be discontinued. Because all known treatments would serve no therapeutic or palliative purpose, they recommended that the infant daughter, soon to be known to the outside world as Baby K, be provided nutrition, hydration, and warmth, and allowed to die.

Again, the mother disagreed. She was firm in her belief "that all life is sacred and must be protected." This included her anencephalic daughter's life. She knew it looked hopeless. She believed God could work miracles. She wanted everything possible done, including the use of the ventilator. Given the profoundly limiting birth defects, the tending physicians remained firm in their belief that continuing their futile efforts was morally and professionally inappropriate.

The final iteration of the *Baby Doe Regulations* contained provisions for terminating treatment when, in the treating physicians' "reasonable medical judgment," any of three circumstances applied: The infant was chronically or irreversibly comatose; the treatment would merely prolong dying, and not be effective in ameliorating or correcting life-threatening conditions; the treatment itself would be inhumane. For one nurse caring for Baby K, it was clear. These conditions were present. "I find it appalling to care for her each day. It is cruel and inhumane to keep her 'alive.' Animals are euthanized for far less problems and yet this is a human being who really has no voice and no rights other than her mother demanding she be kept alive" (quoted in Perkin 1996). Other medical personnel agreed. They turned to the hospital's ethics committee for guidance.

While the committee agreed with the physicians, the impasse with Baby K's mother continued. The hospital then sought to transfer the infant to another hospital. No other hospital would accept responsibility. Costs for hospital care were estimated to be about $1,400 per day. The mother had insurance, but nursing home care would be less expensive. About a month after her birth, the baby's condition stabilized somewhat and her mother agreed to have her daughter transferred to a nearby nursing home. The transfer agreement was reached only after an explicit agreement had been secured that if an emergency with breathing or other functions reoccurred, the hospital would again admit her daughter.

In mid-January 1993, the infant's breathing difficulties again became life threatening. She was returned to the hospital for a month of support. Over the next few months, this back-and-forth transfer between nursing care and hospital occurred a total of three times. Following the second readmission, when the infant was now six months old, the hospital, joined by the guardian *ad litem* and the baby's father, sought, through legal action, to resolve the issue of whether the hospital was obligated to "provide emergency medical treatment to Baby K that it deems medically and ethically inappropriate."

The trial court found that they were. The appellate court agreed, noting that it was "beyond the limits of our judicial function to address the moral and ethical propriety of providing emergency stabilizing medical treatment to anencephalic infants" (*In the Matter of Baby K*. 1993, 1994). The court's findings were not based on an assessment of Baby K's medical condition and treatment, which physicians found futile and ethically inappropriate, but on federal legislation—the Emergency Medical Treatment & Labor Act (EMTALA). This law, also known as the patient anti-dumping law, had been passed by Congress in 1986 to prevent Medicare-participating hospitals from refusing emergency treatment for patients simply because they could not afford it.

Baby K's breathing difficulties constituted an emergency. Parents had the right to request emergency medical treatment for their children. In this case, Baby K's parents disagreed with one another. In such circumstances the court found priority should be given to the decision "in favor of life." The hospital was obligated to provide the requested treatment, regardless of the futility when it came to the baby's more serious underlying medical condition. Baby K lived to be two and one-half years old. Disagreements over whether her short "vegetative" life had been worthy of heroic, expensive, and, ultimately, futile support measures would continue for many years.

Dealing with Futility

The physicians tending Baby K knew the ventilator would prolong her life. They also knew there was no known way to improve the profoundly limiting quality of her life. It was futile to try. The infant's mother disagreed. Her baby's life, even for a few moments, was worth fighting for. The ventilator provided those moments. It was not futile.

The meaning of futile treatment, when applied to particular life circumstances, can become as contentious as it is unclear. In one sense, however, there is absolute clarity. Unless there is a dramatic medical or genetic breakthrough, as of this writing, we will all eventually die, no matter how we might "rage against the dying of the light." There are no exceptions. In this sense, all medical treatment is futile. At the same time, until death occurs nothing is futile. We can always fight for a final moment of life.

What then is the answer? Who should decide? There was a time when "doctor's orders" ruled the day. Trust was high and relations with patients direct and personal. The idea of questioning your doctor and relying instead on third-party review, including hospital ethics committees and litigation, was as remote as it was inappropriate. With increased emphasis on patient autonomy and specialized, sometimes highly technical and costly treatment, this changed.

Instead of close personal relations with their patients, in many ways doctors became "strangers at the bedside;" health care providers whose singular judgment, infused as it is with the uncertainties of rapidly evolving medical technology and treatments with uncertain outcomes, became routinely challenged and frequently reviewed. As David Rothman has noted, "[T]he discretion that the profession once enjoyed has been increasingly circumscribed, with an almost bewildering number of parties and procedures participating in medical decision making" (Rothman 1991: 1).

Such was the case involving a young mother and her infant son who died at the age of 19 months in Austin Texas on May 19, 2007. Emilio Gonzales was born with **Leigh's Disease**, a rare disorder causing the breakdown of his central nervous system and related motor skills. Six months before his death, on December 28, 2006, he was admitted to the local Children's Hospital. By the time he was 17 months old he was in an intensive care unit. He was not, as Baby K had been, vegetative. He was, however, losing his motor skills, he was deaf and blind, and his brain was shrinking. These conditions were getting worse day-by-day. As his condition deteriorated, he could still experience pain.

Efforts to reduce pain and discomfort meant he spent most of his time asleep from the effects of medication. He was kept alive with hydration, nutrition, and a respirator, the removal of which would result, his doctor's estimated, in his death within minutes or hours. While his life could be prolonged, there was no known treatment for the degenerative effects of Leigh's Disease. In this sense, continued treatment was futile. Eventually, as his condition worsened, tending physicians wanted to remove Emilio from the respirator. It was inhumane they felt to do otherwise. Emilio's mother disagreed. She wanted to spend more time with her son. She did not want the timing of her son's death determined by physicians. God would decide.[4]

Eight years earlier, the state of Texas had passed an Advance Directives Act. This legislation, signed into law by then Governor George W. Bush, combined three existing laws, with revisions, into a single law. There were a number of provisions, including

---

4 This case received a good deal of local and national attention. See, "Dying boy's case likely to reverberate in law, religion," 2007, A01; *"Case Puts Texas Futile-Treatment Law Under a Microscope"* 2007, A03; Schultz 2007: A03.

a new living will as well as definitions of terminal and irreversible illness, but the legislation became best known as the Texas Futile Care Law.[5] If a patient requested treatment the physician felt was futile, a seven-step process was outlined to resolve the dispute (Baylor University Medical Center 2000). These steps were patterned after a report of the American Medical Association, released that same year ("Medical futility in end-of-life care" 1999).

Futility was not formally defined in the legislation. If consultation among the family and doctors resulted in disagreement, the dispute was to be taken to a hospital ethics consultation committee. The committee, with the invited participation of the family, was to decide. If disagreement still remained, the hospital, working with the family, was instructed to arrange transfer of the patient to another physician or institution willing to give the treatment requested by the family. Ten days were given for the transfer. At the end of this time, if no physician or hospital could be found, "the hospital and physician may unilaterally withhold or withdraw therapy that has been determined to be futile."

As a last resort, the dispute could be taken to court for an extension of the 10-day deadline. The extension was to be granted if the judge determined there is a reasonable likelihood of finding a willing provider of the disputed treatment. If the family decided not to seek an extension or the judge failed to grant one, "futile treatment may be unilaterally withdrawn by the treatment team with immunity from civil and criminal prosecution."

This was the situation Emilio Gonzales's mother and the hospital and health care providers confronted. The consultation process had been completed. No agreement had been reached. The 10-day deadline had been passed. It had been extended once. A county judge had been persuaded to extend it again while a search continued, but a federal judge declined to intervene. Thirty-one facilities had been contacted with no success. For her part, Emilio's mother remained firm in her belief and wishes, "I believe there is a hospital that is going to accept my son.... I just want to spend time with my son.... I want to let him die naturally without someone coming up and saying we're going to cut off on a certain day" (Morena 2007: A03).

Advocacy groups seeking stronger rights for the disabled developed petitions and wrote the Texas governor, asking for a "stay of execution" of young Emilio. The Texas legislature, which convenes every other year, was in session. A revised law was drafted. It provided more time to find alternative treatment. As the debate wore on, young Emilio's condition worsened and he died while the legislature was in session, held by his mother in the last moments of his life. The revised legislation floundered in the

---

5 See the *Advance Directives Act* 1999, Chapter 166 of the Texas Health & Safety Code, especially Section 166.046, Subsection (e).

2007 legislative session. It was reintroduced in 2009. Once again, it failed to emerge from committee hearings (House Bill 3325).

Futility involves both objective and subjective judgments. What is the time horizon sought—a year, a month, a day, a moment? What is the quality of life desired—restoration of function, an acceptable sense of self, a level of consciousness, the absence of pain or suffering? What are the chances that the desired outcome, whatever that might be, can be achieved? When numbers are used, is medical treatment futile if there is a very high probability (scientists like to talk about five nines—99.999%) that the procedure or treatment will not accomplish the ends sought. Even using the five-9s criterion, however, there is one chance in 100,000 that something might work. Why not try?

The improbable might become real. "[H]ope is what human beings summon up to seek a miracle against overwhelming odds. It is possible then to say in the same breath, 'I know this is futile, but I have hope'" (Schneiderman, Jecker, and Jonsen 1990: 950). A sense of futility comes when all hope is gone to achieve an acceptable quality of life.

Dealing with Uncertainty

Potential, by definition, remains unclear. Making decisions with uncertain, differentially valued potential for life is never an easy task.[6] There are uncertainties, even with such clearly debilitating conditions as anencephaly, Leigh's Disease, spina bifida, hydrocephaly, and microcephaly. How extensively will mental capacities be diminished? How long is life likely to last? How much suffering will be endured?

There are also uncertainties of intentions embedded in such principles as the **Doctrine of Double Effect**—intending good, knowing harm will follow—so widely discussed by philosophers and lawyers. Are drugs being administered to hasten death, to alleviate suffering, or both? Setting these questions aside, when there is a single-minded intention to let life go, even to hasten its end, this may reflect care, palliative healing, virtue, compassion, and justice. It may also reflect neglect and abuse, or perhaps a judgment that individual interests should be set aside for the greater good. The sanctity of *LIFE* should be protected, no matter the individual consequences, to prevent the emergence of a culture of death.

Finally, there are uncertainties of who should decide. The infant's wishes are not known. "[I]t is nonsensical in general secular terms to speak of respecting the autonomy of fetuses, infants, or profoundly retarded adults, who have never been rational. There is no autonomy to affront" (Engelhardt, Jr. 1996: 139). Attention turns

---

6 For arguments from potential in other bioethical settings see Singer and Dawson 1988: 87–104 and Reichlin 1997: 1–23.

to those closest to the infant. How much weight should be given to assessments of quality-of-life preferences when compared to the inherent value of *LIFE*, regardless of individual interests and preferences? Mothers, fathers, other relatives, doctors, nurses, surrogates, lawyers, government officials, and judges all have standing. They also frequently have competing preferences, interests, and intentions. Fully satisfying, consensus-generating boundaries of protected life and tension-free resolution of the embedded dilemmas remain elusive, perhaps unachievable.

DISCUSSION QUESTIONS

1. Describe the challenges associated with determining a disabled child's "quality of life."
2. The withholding of care of a disabled infant is described in competing ways. Describe these competing perspectives.
3. What is the "monster" analogy? How does describing a disabled infant in this way impact our ability to empathize with the child?
4. Who should have the right to make the final call about a disabled infants care? The parents? Hospital personnel? State legislatures? The federal government?
5. What is your opinion on the Emilio Gonzales case? Should the hospital have been required to provide continued care for Emilio?
6. Take the position that parents of disabled infants should be punished if they refuse medical care for their child. What would be an appropriate punishment for such cases?
7. Describe the concept of "futility" as it applies to disabled infants. What are the challenges associated with determining futility?
8. What is the Doctrine of Double Effect and how does it apply to the debate over care of disabled infants?

Bibliography

The Advance Directives Act. (1999). Chapter 166 of the Texas Health & Safety Code, Section 166.046, Subsection (e).

Annas, George. 1984. "The Case of Baby Jane Doe: Child Abuse or Unlawful Federal Intervention?" *American Journal of Public Health 74*: 727–29.

———. 1994. "Asking the Courts to Set the Standard of Emergency Care — The Case of Baby K." *New England Journal of Medicine 330*: 1542–45.

Apgar, Virginia. 1969. "Statement by Virginia Agpar to Subcommittee on Health, Senate Committee on Labor and Public Welfare, June 30." Retrieved June 23, 2011 (http://profiles.nlm.nih.gov/ps/retrieve/ResourceMetadata/CPBBGK).

Arkes, Hadley, Robert Bork, Charles Colson, Robert George, and Russell Hittinger. 1996. *Symposium: The End of Democracy? Judicial Usurpation of Politics.* Retrieved June 23, 2011 (http://www.firstthings.com/issue/1996/11/november).

The Army of God. N.D. "George Tiller-The Baby Killer." Retrieved June 23, 2011 (http://www.armyofgod.com/GeorgeTillerBabyKillerIndex.html).

Baylor University Medical Center. 2000. "Guidelines for Resolving Futility Cases under the Texas Advance Directives Act, 1999." *Proceedings 13*(2): 144–47.

Becker, Howard. 1963. *Outsiders: Studies in the Sociology of Deviance.* Glencoe, IL: The Free Press of Glencoe.

Bird, David. 1983. "U.S. Role In 'Baby Doe' Case Defended By Surgeon General." *New York Times,* November 7. Retrieved June 23, 2011 (http://www.nytimes.com/1983/11/07/nyregion/us-role-in-baby-doe-case-defended-by-surgeon-general.html).

Blanchard, Dallas A. 1994. *The Anti-Abortion Movement and the Rise of the Religious Right.* New York: Twayne Publishers.

Blanchard, Dallas A., and T. J. Prewitt. 1993. *Religious Violence and Abortion: The Gideon Project.* Gainesville: University Press of Florida.

Booth, William. 1993. "Doctor Killed During Abortion Protest." *Washington Post* (March 11: A01).

Bowen v. American Hosp. Ass'n, 476 U. S. 610 (1986): 621, 632

Bray, et al., Petitioners v. Alexandria Women's Health Clinic, et al., 506 U.S. 263 (1993).

Brown, Lawrence. 1986. "Civil Rights and Regulatory Wrongs: The Reagan Administration and the Medical Treatment of Handicapped Infants." *Journal of Health Politics, Policy and Law 11*: 234–54.

Chambers, Marcia. 1983. "Initiator of 'Baby Doe' Case Unshaken." *New York Times* (November 13). Retrieved June 23, 2011 (http://www.nytimes.com/1983/11/13/nyregion/initiator-of-baby-doe-case-unshaken.html).

Dorfman, Sally Faith, Hart Peterson, William Rashbaum, Seymour L. Romney, Allan Rosenfield, Herbert G. Vaughan, Jr., and Ming-NengYeh. 2002. "White Paper: The Facts Speak Louder than 'The Silent Scream'." New York: Planned Parenthood. Retrieved June 23, 2011 (http://www.plannedparenthood.org/files/PPFA/Facts_Speak_Louder_than_the_Silent_Scream_03-02.pdf).

Duffy, Edward. 1971. *The Effects of Changes in the State Abortion Laws.* Washington, D.C.: U.S. Department of Health, Education, and Welfare, Public Health Service.

Dworkin, Ronald. 1993. *Life's Dominion: An Argument About Abortion, Euthanasia, and Individual Freedom.* New York: Alfred A. Knopf.

"Dying Boy's Case Likely to Reverberate in Law, Religion." 2007. *Austin American Statesman* (April 15: A01).

Dynak, Hadley. 1953. Honoring San Francisco's Abortion Pioneers — A Celebration of Past and Present Medical Public Health Leadership. San Francisco: Center for Reproductive Health Research & Policy.

Eisenstadt v. Baird, 405 U.S. 438 (1972) 405 U.S. 438

Eckholm, Eric. 2001 "Several States Forbid Abortion after 20 Weeks." *New York Times* (June 26). Retrieved July 5, 2011 (http://www.nytimes.com/2011/06/27/us/27abortion.html?hp).

Ekland-Olson, Sheldon. 2012. *Who Lives, Who Dies, Who Decides?* New York: Routledge.

Ely, John Hart. 1973. "The Wages of Crying Wolf: A Comment on *Roe v. Wade.*" *Yale Law Journal* 82: 920–49.

Engelhardt, H. Tristram Jr. 1996. *The Foundations of Bioethics* (2nd ed.). New York: Oxford University Press.

Fiorina, Morris P., Samuel J. Abrams, and Jeremy C. Pope. 2006. *Culture War? The Myth of a Polarized America.* New York: Pearson Longman.

Fletcher, Joseph. 1954. *Morals and Medicine.* Princeton: Princeton University Press.

The Forerunner. 1987. "Rescue Mission at Cherry Hill Abortion Clinic." Retrieved June 23, 2011 (http://forerunner.com/forerunner/X0425_Cherry_Hill_Rescue.html).

——— 1998. "Randall Terry Interview." Retrieved June 23, 2011 (http://forerunner.com/forerunner/X0471_Randall_Terry_Interv.html).

Freedom of Access to Clinics Entrances (FACE) Act–or the Access Act, Pub. L. No. 103-259, 108 Stat. 694) (May 26, 1994, 18 U.S.C. § 248)

Goldberg, Carey. 2007. "Shots Assist in Aborting Fetuses; Lethal Injections Offer Legal Shield." *Boston Globe* (August 10). Retrieved March 2009 (http://www.boston.com/news/local/articles/2007/08/10/shots_assist_in_aborting_fetuses)

Gonzales v. Carhart, 550 U.S. 124 (2007).

Gorney, Cynthia. 2004. "Gambling with Abortion: Why Both Sides Think They Have Everything to Lose." *Harper's Magazine* (November). Retrieved June 23, 2011 (http://harpers.org/archive/2004/11/0080278).

Greenhouse, Linda. 2005. *Becoming Justice Blackmun: Harry Blackmun's Supreme Court Journey.* New York: Times Books.

Griswold v. Connecticut, 381 U.S. 479 (1965).

Halfmann, Drew. "Historical Priorities and the Response of Doctors' Associations to Abortion Reform Proposals in Britain and the United States, 1960–1973." *Social Problems 50*: 567–91.

Haskell, Martin. 1992. "Dilation and Extraction for Late Second Trimester Abortion." Presentation at the National Abortion Federation Risk Management Seminar, September 13.

Hittinger, Russell. 1996. "A Crisis of Legitimacy." *First Things 67* (November): 25–29.

Horsley, Neal. 2001. "Understanding the Army of God." Retrieved June 23, 2011 (http://www.christiangallery.com/aog.html).

Hunter, James Davison. 1991. *Cultural Wars: The Struggle to Define America.* New York: Basic Books.

Hyde, Henry. 1996. "Henry Hyde's Plea to Override President Clinton's Veto of the Partial-Birth Abortion Ban." National Right to Life Committee. Retrieved June 23, 2011 (http://www.nrlc.org/news/2003/NRL01/index.html).

Iglesias, Teresa. 1984. "In Vitro Fertilization: The Major Issues." *Journal of Medical Ethics 10*: 32–37.

In the Matter of Baby K, 832 F. Supp. 1022 (E.D. Va. 1993).

In the Matter of Baby K, 16 F.3d 590 (4th Cir. 1994).

Joffe, Carole E., Tracy A. Weitz, and C. L. Stacey. 2004. "Uneasy Allies: Pro-choice Physicians, Feminist Health Activists and the Struggle for Abortion Rights." *Sociology of Health and Illness 26*: 775–96.

Kadish, Sanford. 1999. "Fifty Years of Criminal Law: An Opinionated Review." *California Law Review 87*(4): 943–82.

Katz, Esther, Cathy Moran Hajo, and Peter C. Engelman, eds. 2003. *The Selected Papers of Margaret Sanger.* Urbana: University of Illinois Press.

"Killing Abortionists: A Symposium." 1994. *First Things 48*: 24–31.

Kinsley, Michael. 1994. "Why Not Kill the Baby Killers?" *Time Magazine* (August 15). Retrieved June 23, 2011 (http://www.time.com/time/magazine/article/0,9171,981276,00.html).

Ku Klux Klan Act or the Civil Rights Act of 1871 (17 Stat. 13).

Kuhse, Helga, and Peter Singer. 1985. *Should the Baby Live? The Problem of Handicapped Infants.* Oxford: Oxford University Press.

Levin, Marc, and Daphne Pinkerson. 2000. *Soldiers in the Army of God.* New York: HBO Video.

Luker, Kristin. 1984. *Abortion and the Politics of Motherhood.* Berkeley: University of California Press.

"Medical Futility in End-of-Life Care: Report of the Council on Ethical and Judicial Affairs." 1999. *Journal of the American Medical Association 281*: 937–41.

Moreno, Sylvia. 2007. "Case Puts Texas Futile-Treatment Law under a Microscope." *Washington Post* (April 11: A03).

"The Nashville Statement of Conscience—The Struggle Against Abortion: Why the Use of Lethal Force is Not Morally Justifiable." 1994. Retrieved June 23, 2011 (http://erlc.com/article/nashville-declaration-of-conscience/).

Nathanson, Bernard. 1996. *The Hand of God: A Journey from Death to Life by the Abortion Doctor who Changed His Mind.* Washington, D.C.: Regnery Publishing.

Nicholas, Jude. 2000. "Congenital Rubella Syndrome, Neuropsychological Functioning and Implications Illustrated by a Case Study." Denmark: Nordic Staff Training Center for Deafblind Services.

North, Gary. 1994. *Lone Gunners for Jesus: Letters to Paul J. Hill*. Tyler, TX: Institute for Christian Economics.

Office of the Clark County Prosecuting Attorney. N.D. "Paul Jennings Hill." Retrieved June 23, 2011 (http://www.clarkprosecutor.org/html/death/US/hill873.htm).

"Partial Birth Abortion." N.D. Retrieved June 23, 2011 (http://mikeaustin.org/AAA/Partial%20Birth%20Abortion/PartialBirthAbortion.jpg).

The Partial-Birth Abortion Ban Act of 2003 (Pub. L. 108-105, HR 760, S 3, 18 U.S. Code 1531).

People v. Belous, 71 Cal.2d 954, 458 P.2d 194, 80 Cal.Rptr. 354 (1969).

Perkin, Ronald. 1996. "Stress and Distress in Pediatric Nurses: The Hidden Tragedy of Baby K." Retrieved June 23, 2011 (http://www.llu.edu/llu/bioethics/update12_2.htm).

Planned Parenthood of Southeastern Pennsylvania v. Casey, 505 U.S. 833 (1992)

Pope Paul VI. 1968. "On the Regulation of Birth." *Humanae Vitae Encyclical* (July 25).

Pratt Shafer, Brenda. "Hearing on Partial Birth Abortion. Testimony of Brenda Pratt Shafer, Subcommittee on the Constitution, U.S. House of Representatives, March 21, 1996." Retrieved June 23, 2011 (http://judiciary.house.gov/legacy/215.htm).

Prolife Action League. N.D. "Conduct Your Own Truth Tour." Retrieved June 23, 2011 (http://prolifeaction.org/truth/howto.htm).

———. N.D. "Sidewalk Counseling." Retrieved June 23, 2011 (http://prolifeaction.org/sidewalk/packet.htm).

Ramsey, Paul. 1978. *Ethics at the Edges of Life*. New Haven: Yale University Press.

Reagan, Leslie. 1997. *When Abortion was a Crime: Women, Medicine, and Law in the United States, 1867–1973*. Berkeley: University of California Press.

Reagan, Ronald. 1983. "Abortion and the Conscience of the Nation." *The Human Life Review*. Retrieved in June 22, 2011 (http://humanlifereview.com).

Reichlin, Massimo. 1997. "The Argument from Potential: A Reappraisal." *Bioethics 11*: 1–23.

Reiman, Jeffrey. 1999. *Abortion and the Ways We Value Human Life*. New York: Rowman & Littlefield.

Risen, James, and Judy L. Thomas. 1988. *Wrath of Angles: The American Abortion War*. New York: Basic Books.

Rohter, Larry. 1994. "Towering Over the Abortion Foe's Trial: His Leader." *New York Times* (March 5). Retrieved June 23, 2011 (http://www.nytimes.com/1994/03/05/us/towering-over-the-abortion-foe-s-trial-his-leader.html).

Rothman, David J. 1991. *Strangers at the Bedside: A History of How Law and Bioethics Transformed Medical Decision Making*. New York: Aldine de Gruyter.

Rudolph, Eric. N.D. "Eric Rudolph's Homepage." Retrieved June 23, 2011 (http://www.armyofgod.com/EricRudolphHomepage.html).

Saad, Lydia. 2002. "Public Opinion About Abortion—An In-Depth Review." *The Gallup Poll: Public Opinion 2002*. Retrieved June 23, 2011 (http://www.gallup.com/poll/9904/public-opinion-about-abortion-indepth-review.aspx#3).

Sauer, R. 1974. "Attitudes to Abortion in America, 1800–1973." *Population Studies 28*: 53–67.

Schaeffer, Francis. 1981. *A Christian Manifesto*. Westchester, IL: Crossway Books.

Schneiderman, L. J., N. S. Jecker, and A. R. Jonsen. 1990. "Medical Futility: Its Meaning and Ethical Implications." *Annals of Internal Medicine 112*: 949–54.

"2nd Trimester Abortion: An Interview with W. Martin Haskell, MD." 1993. *Cincinnati Medicine* Fall: 18–19.

The Silent Scream. Retrieved September 2009 (http://www.silentscream.org/silent_e.htm).

Singer, Peter. 1993. *Practical Ethics*. Cambridge: Cambridge University Press.

Singer, Peter, and Karen Dawson. 1988. "Technology and the Argument from Potential." *Philosophy and Public Affairs 17*: 87–104.

Smith, Wesley. 2000. *Culture of Death: The Assault on Medical Ethics in America*. San Francisco: Encounter Books.

Spitz, Donald. N.D. "The Unedited Version of Paul Hill's Book: Mix My Blood with the Blood of the Unborn." Retrieved June 23, 2011 (http://www.armyofgod.com/PHillbookIntro.html).

Stenberg v. Carhart 530 U.S. 914 (2000).

Tooley, Michael. 1972. "Abortion and Infanticide." *Philosophy & Public Affairs 2*: 37–65.

Van Den Haag, Ernest Washington, and Lacey Washington. 1984. "Baby Jane Doe." *National Review* (February 10: 36–38).

Veritas, Sandy. N.D. "George Tiller was a Mass-Murderer, says Randall Terry — We Grieve That he Did Not Have Time to Properly Prepare His Soul to Face God." *Christian News Wire*. Retrieved June 23, 2011 (http://www.christiannewswire.com/news/8967610531.html).

Voss, Gretchen. 2004. "My Late Term Abortion." *Boston Globe* (January 25). Retrieved June 23, 2011 (http://www.boston.com/news/globe/magazine/articles/2004/01/25/my_late_term_abortion/).

Watson, J. 1973. "Children from the Laboratory." *American Medical Association Prism* May: 13.

Will, George F. 1982. "The Killing Will Not Stop." *The Washington Post* (April 22: A29).

Williams, Glanville. 1957. *The Sanctity of Life and the Criminal Law*. New York: Alfred A. Knopf.

Glossary/Index

A

A Time to Kill: A Study Concerning the Use of Force and Abortion (Bray, et al.) 34

abortion

    late-term 2, 20, 34, 36, 37, 38, 39, 42, 47

    partial-birth 34, 35, 38, 39, 40, 41, 42–43, 47

    therapeutic abortion committees 7, 9, 10

Abortion (Lader) 12

abortion on demand: the ability of a woman to decide to terminate her pregnancy for any reason 11, 13, 18, 21, 39

Act for the Suppression of Trade in, and Circulation of, Obscene Literature and Articles for Immoral Use 4

Advance Directives Act (Texas) 59

Alabama 27, 30, 32, 46

ALI (American Law Institute) 9, 10, 13, 15

ALL (American Life League) 22

American Academy of Pediatrics 53

American Birth Control Movement 4

American Hospital Association 53, 56, 69

American Medical Association 60

anencephaly: a child is born missing a large part of the brain and skull 56, 61

anthrax 29

Arizona 1, 7–8, 9

Army of God 29–31, 33

Assembly of God Church 23, 27

B

Baby Doe 36, 51, 53

Baby Doe Guidelines/Regulations: Federal regulations implemented in 1985 requiring that disabled infants with life-threatening conditions receive appropriate nutrition, hydration, and medication, according to the treating physician's reasonable medical judgment that such treatment is most likely to be effective in ameliorating or correcting all such conditions. Parents who refuse care can be charged with child abuse. 54, 56, 57

fetus
　　and abortion procedures 35–36, 37, 40
　　and late-term abortions 33
　　and legal protections 2, 11
　　and *No Greater Joy* 22–23
　　and partial birth abortion ban 42, 43, 46
　　and *Roe v. Wade* 15–16, 18
　　and self-awareness 35–36
　　and *Silent Scream* 21
　　and Thalidomide 8, 14
　　and viability 19–20

Hussein, Saddam 28
Hyde, Henry 38
hydrocephaly: fluid accumulates in the brain, sometimes causing brain damage 54, 61

I
Illinois 10, 23
incest 9, 10, 14, 21, 46
Indiana 46, 50, 51, 53
induction 39
infusion 39
Interim Final Rule 53

J
Johnson, Douglas 37

K
Kansas 26, 28, 29, 34, 46
Kennedy, Anthony 25, 44, 45
Koop, C. Everett 55, 56
Ku Klux Klan Act of 1871 26, 29
Kuhse, Helga 49, 50, 53

L
Lader, Lawrence 12
late-term abortion 2, 20, 34, 36, 37, 38, 39, 42, 47
Leigh's Disease: a rare disorder causing the breakdown of the central nervous system and related motor skills 59, 61
Luker, Kristin 13

M
Massachusetts 5, 32, 46
Mexico 11
Mix My Blood with the Blood of the Unborn (Hill) 31–32
"monster" metaphor 52–53, 62
moral entrepreneur 4
moral imperative: a widely and deeply held belief that governs the ways in which human beings should behave 1
Moral Majority 26
Morals and Medicine (Fletcher) 52
MPC (Model Penal Code) 9, 13, 18

and death threats 23–24
and *Doe v. Bolton* 20
and fetus 2
and legal penumbras 5, 6, 7, 13, 20, 25
and *Roe v. Wade* 12–13, 16–17, 25
and *Stenberg* decision 40–41, 43, 44, 45, 46
United States v. Vuitch 12

V

viability: the point at which the fetus is capable of meaningful life outside the mother's womb 1, 19, 20, 25, 33, 36, 46, 48, 53
Virginia 32, 56
Voss, Gretchen 42
Vuitch, Milan 12

W

Washburn, Lawrence, Jr. 54, 55, 56
Watson, James 49
Webster v. Reproductive Health Services 25
Westberg, Jenny 37
Wichita, Kansas 26–27, 28, 34
Will, George 51, 52, 56
Will, Jonathan 51, 53
Williams, Glanville 52

Y

Yale Law Journal 16
Younger v. Harris 15